MW00629892

VIOLENCE IN MODERN PHILOSOPHY

VIOLENCE IN MODERN PHILOSOPHY

Piotr Hoffman

The University of Chicago Press
Chicago and London

PIOTR HOFFMAN is professor of philosophy at the
University of Nevada, Reno. His previous books
include *Doubt, Time, Violence,* also published by the
University of Chicago Press.

The University of Chicago Press, Chicago 60637
The University of Chicago Press, Ltd., London
© 1989 by The University of Chicago
All rights reserved. Published 1989
Printed in the United States of America
98 97 96 95 94 93 92 91 90 89   54321

Library of Congress Cataloging-in-Publication Data
Hoffman, Piotr.
  Violence in modern philosophy / Piotr Hoffman.
    p. cm.
  Bibliography: p.
  Includes index.
  ISBN 0-226-34795-8 (alk. paper)
  1. Violence. 2. Philosophy, Modern. 3. Knowledge, Theory of.
I. Title.
B844.H65 1989
128'.4—dc19   88-34125
                                               CIP

⊗The paper used in this publication meets
the minimum requirements of the American National
Standard for Information Sciences—Permanence of
Paper for Printed Library Materials, ANSI
Z39.48-1984.

CONTENTS

PREFACE

The political philosophy with which the modern age begins—the thinking of Machiavelli and Hobbes—focuses upon a constant possibility of violence threatening the life of human communities. Violence looms at the horizon of escalating social conflicts and antagonisms; violence is the very counterpart of the inherent fragility of human communities which, unlike physical phenomena, are sustained in existence not by the operation of some natural laws but by a precarious social consensus, vulnerable to disintegration and collapse. Thus a philosophical reflection upon man's social and political life must, inevitably, take into account and come to terms with the reality and the experience of human violence. It would be more than surprising, though, if this crucial role of the notion of violence were to be limited to modern political philosophy alone. For philosophy in general is, at least to some degree, shaped by the experiences and the thoughts of human agents as they interact with each other in their communities; and so, we may presume, a way of life which found its expression in the political thinking of Machiavelli and Hobbes would be more than likely to have left its impact upon other areas of philosophical inquiry. And since that way of life was characterized by, among other things, man's acute awareness of the ever-present possibility of violence, then, we may guess, this life experience must have filtered into human attempts to articulate the world in philosophical categories.

I have already had the opportunity to substantiate this claim in some respects.* For example, I have argued that Descartes' problematic of doubt—an important part of our own philosophical problematic, as we continue to be preoccupied by the issue of philosophical skepticism—is indeed reflective of man's exposure to a violent world, since Descartes' "evil demon," whose threatening presence makes one doubt all of one's beliefs and certainties, is in fact the personification of the human

---

*See my recent book *Doubt, Time, Violence* (Chicago: University of Chicago Press, 1986); see too, an earlier study of mine, *The Human Self and the Life and Death Struggle* (Gainesville/Tampa: University Presses of Florida, 1983).

threats confronting an individual in an environment of violence. A similar account, I have argued, is demanded by the notion of human temporality and by a number of other philosophical issues. The present study is meant to continue the same line of investigation.

The pivotal notion remains the notion of *the other* as the *ultimate limit* of one's powers. In effect, our practically accomplished mastery of the natural environment has left intact the limitation of human agents by each other. As a member of my own species, the other is in possession of powers and capacities that are essentially similar, and equal to, my own; and hence *his* threat to me is in principle beyond my control. Thus the very same forces of science and technology that allow me to master nature may always be turned against me by the other. In a violent environment the other emerges as an insurmountable obstacle to my aims and purposes, or else as an inescapable danger which I am powerless to hold at bay. In this sense, he is the focus of an ultimate *resistance* to my powers.

I shall continue to argue that this very special status of the other as the ultimate limit of one's powers is at the root of several key notions around which modern philosophy has built its problematic. I shall argue that when this violent background of modern philosophizing is taken into account various conceptual tensions and puzzles can receive satisfying solutions. Since I do not believe in any "architectonic" of thinking, I have no way of justifying beforehand the selection of the material to be discussed in the present study. I trust, however, that a glance at the table of contents will convince the reader of the importance of that material to philosophical reflection in general. I hope that initial impression will be strengthened as the reader makes his way through the book.

One final word to explain the somewhat different character of the two chapters of the book. Whereas Chapter I deals with the issues, the texts, and the philosophers that will be familiar to many readers, Chapter II concentrates on the problematic of Hegel's *Logic*. The difficulty and the obscurity of Hegel's writing in general and of his *Science of Logic* in particular have by now become a legend of their own. And so I thought it advisable to provide the readers with a detailed commentary on the Hegelian text I will be analyzing, to support my claim about the key role that the notion of violence plays in his philosophy as well. Needless to say, it was not possible to circumvent that philosophy. For Hegel's system was, and remains, the crowning point, not only of modern philosophy, but indeed of the entire Western philosophical tradition. Most of what took place after Hegel represents either some attempt at "overcoming" or "dissolving" that tradition, or else a more or less obvious throwback to the pre-Hegelian positions.

I would like to take this opportunity to express my thanks to Hubert L. Dreyfus, Charles B. Guignon, Andrzej Rapaczynski, and an anonymous reader for the University of Chicago Press for conveying to me a number of valuable comments and criticisms which contributed to shape the final version of the book.

ABBREVIATIONS

Works frequently cited in the text and notes have been abbreviated. Full bibliographic information is available in the list of works cited which follows the notes at the end of the book.

SL   G. W. F. Hegel, *Hegel's Science of Logic*
Enc.   G. W. F. Hegel, *The Encyclopaedia of the Philosophical Sciences,* parts I, II, III
CPR I. Kant, *Critique of Pure Reason*

I.

THE OPENING MOVES

I.

The Thing and its Properties

The notion of the *thing* is basic to our natural, prephilosophical attitude—we encounter things both in our practical commerce with the world and in our perceptual exploration of it—and it at once presents the philosopher with an immediate and truly colossal challenge. The thing is a unity and a multiplicity, a one and a many. The thing "has" or "is" its many properties, it is qualified by them; while, conversely, the properties are viewed not as free-floating items but as belonging to the thing in question.

The diversity of properties qualifies the thing as object of one sense but also, and even especially, as object of several senses; as an intersensorial unit—as an entity perceivable by sight, by touch, and so on—the thing appears as a multiplicity of properties: the thing is colored, hard, odorous, and so on. At a further stage of analysis one may want to raise a more sophisticated question as to whether the contribution of this or that sense does or does not truly enrich our conception of the thing. Whatever may be the answer, though, the thing remains an intersensorial unit endowed, due to this fact alone, with a multiplicity of properties. But even a thing's appearance to one sense presents us with the coexistence of unity and multiplicity. A thing may have several colors, or its color may have several shades, or one and the same shade will be spread over different parts of the thing's surface, and so on. In all of these cases we shall not hesitate for a moment in attributing the multiplicity of properties to the thing in question.

But what do we attribute these properties to? Every property is conceived as being property *of* something. Clearly, then, that to which we attribute them all cannot itself be a further property. Were this to be the case, then the latter, in turn, would have to be ascribed to something still further and other than itself. For example, if I ascribe this green color to this surface and if I construe the surface as being itself a property, then I quite naturally interpret it as qualifying this apple; it is the apple, then, which functions as the owner of both the color and the surface.

1

Were I to refrain from considering the surface as being the surface of an apple, I would soon find myself confronted with a surface which—strangely enough—takes over the functions belonging to a thing. The surface would begin to behave like a thing in its own right, endowed with its own multitude of properties, perhaps with its own life history and so on. And what this all means is that when I construe properties as being properties of a thing I cannot escape the thought that the thing is something over and above its properties; or to put it differently, being that which "supports" or "has" its properties, the thing cannot be identical with them. Or, again, the thing is *not* its properties, for it is their "bearer," or their "owner," or the "substance" in which they "inhere."

These terms are all borrowed from the standard philosophical vocabulary, but their use is tantamount to the emergence of a paradox. For if the bearer or the substance is not identical with its properties, then where and how are we to find it and to identify it? The green belongs to the surface and the surface belongs to the apple. But where do I find the apple? I see only the green color, the size, and the shape; I smell the fragrance in my nostrils and feel the coolness and the smoothness on the tips of my fingers. At no point do I discover the substance or the bearer to which these properties belong. There is nothing "over and above" the properties. The thing, it turns out, just *is* its properties. Moreover, there is nothing special or unique about these properties; there is no reason, that is, why I should confine them to the boundaries of what I took to be *this* thing. Until now, of course, there seemed to be a reason, and a good one at that: this green color was different from all similar samples of green because, unlike them, it belonged to this particular apple. It was, as it were, the private property of one particular owner. But its owner has now disappeared. All I find is a group of properties, and each of these properties, it appears, has a life of its own, beyond the boundaries of the group. It is the same green that I perceive "here" and "there" and "there." The same green appears in several groupings of properties; it is, we may say, *shared* by several such groupings. Such a shared property is a "universal" and so the thing itself is now nothing but an intersection, or a "bundle" of such universal properties. The thing itself has disappeared.

But perhaps the reason why we have ended up with the

bundle-of-properties notion of the thing might have something to do with the case we have selected for analysis. For the most part, what I did was to simply look at the apple; even when I touched it I did so out of curiosity and sheer desire to explore the thing. I did not, that is, consider the thing as a target of my action and manipulation; my attitude was contemplative through and through. But now suppose I want to *do* something with this or that thing. When I thus abandon the contemplative, detached attitude I suddenly discover the *power* of the thing to resist me. If I want to reduce the size of the desk the apples are on—the desk takes up too much space in my study—I have no choice but to pick an axe or a saw and to force the change in the desk by exerting an effort. Thus the properties of the desk are not, as of now, brought together as a mere bundle. They are bound up by a force that the thing represents; and this dynamic bond of theirs remains essential to them for as long as I don't step over to the disengaged, contemplative attitude. The desk is still the meeting place of several universal properties; but, at the same time, they are particularized by their belonging to the thing viewed as *this* particular causal power.

However, our move away from contemplation of and towards action upon the *things* in our environment will not change the basic facts of the situation. The desk offers a resistance to my aims, but it does conform to them in the end: I *do* succeed, at some point, in chopping off the encumbering part of the desk. I thus—literally and not simply in imagination and in thought—"take apart" the properties of the desk. My ability to imagine or to think the properties apart from their owner and vice versa (I imagine the apple as red and not green; and I imagine the same green spread over that large desk; I then imagine the desk itself as changing its size and becoming small) is in full conformity with my practical ability to follow up on such thought-experiments. My active commerce with the things, therefore, does not yield a conception in which my earlier, incompatible commitments—to the properties, but also to the thing as *this* particular item—can be reconciled. As I now practically demonstrate, the thing *is* a group of properties which can be separated from each other and which are not at all confined to the thing in question.

We have started out by considering properties to be the

properties of a particular thing; we have ended up by holding that the thing is, in fact, only a "cluster" or a "bundle" of properties.

But this last sentence is fraught with danger and, it quickly turns out, we can avoid this danger only by returning to the position we have been forced to abandon. In effect, a universal—or general—property is applicable, by its very nature qua universal, to several particular things. This is how we usually come to be familiar with such properties—we see the same shade of golden-green on many apples of the Golden Delicious variety, etc.—and once we achieve the mastery of thinking such properties and using them in judgments, we understand that any such property may be instantiated (in principle, if not in fact) in several items. But then, once again, these items cease to be particular and become "all alike." Naturally, we may try—and sometimes, even if not often or as a rule, we do try—to recapture that particularity by multiplying the attribution of different, and ever more specific, properties. But it is also easy to see why we must inevitably fail. Our heaping up of properties can in no way secure our ability to pick out just one particular item. No matter how far we go in this exercise, the accumulating bundle of properties will remain a bundle of *general* properties. True, within the whole class of the Golden Delicious only some apples happen to be sour; it nevertheless remains the case that sourness too is a general property which continues to characterize many apples of this variety. And while even fewer of them will be sour *and* rotten, such a combination too may very easily apply to several apples. Neither will we fare any better when we concentrate on just one selected property—say, the golden-green color of the Golden Delicious variety—and attempt to arrange all particular items by their reference to some scale of order and measurement (for example, we could pick one apple as the darkest golden-green, then another apple as the second darkest, and so on). For the properties so arranged remain general nevertheless, and so while we may be successful in individuating apples belonging to *this* heap, there is no reason to believe that other heaps (which we would then also have to individuate) do not contain apples with exactly the same shade of golden-green; all those apples, therefore, would be indistinguishable in terms of their mere position on our scale of order and measurement.

Thus whether we keep piling up or ordering (general) properties we do not reach the particular (thing). We are thus forced to admit that we were right after all, when we thought that the thing qua particular has or is something over and above its properties—that it is their (particular and unique) "bearer."

We will not be prepared to abandon this conclusion as a result of a suggestion to consider the hypothetical limiting case in which the enumeration of a thing's properties would be completed to the last and most minute detail. For even then there would be no reason to believe that such a detailed—indeed infinitely detailed—description of a thing in terms of general properties would pick out just one particular item and that item only. Our refusal to go along with the suggestion put forward is motivated by the shaky status of the *principle of the identity of indiscernibles*. Unless the principle is a necessary truth our refusal is on sound grounds. For if we deny the status of a necessary truth to the principle of the identity of indiscernibles—if we say that several different things could have exactly the same properties, no matter how detailed a set of these properties we would consider—it will follow that different things must be, after all, distinguishable by something over and above the properties which they possess. We could not escape the consequences of this repudiation of the principle of the identity of indiscernibles even if our particular entities were to be viewed as groups of properties combined by a *law* and/or as located in a determinate *spatial* position.[1]

Now, Leibniz's famous principle cannot be proved to be true by virtue of logical necessity. When pressed by Clarke to clarify his position and to supply the proof of the principle, Leibniz hesitates and vacillates. At times he suggests that the principle is indeed logically necessary,[2] but the suggestion is not followed up by a proof. Conversely, when Leibniz does attempt to prove the principle, the proof is based entirely on the assumption that God, in his wisdom, would not go along with the possibility (contrary to the principle of sufficient reason) of creating two indiscernible beings;[3] but the conception of two indiscernibles "seems indeed to be possible in abstract terms"[4]—and this implies that such a possibility is not at all meaningless or logically contradictory. Two hundred and fifty years after Leibniz, a prominent logical analyst will confess, with an understandable sadness, that his own decision to view the principle of the identity of indiscernibles as logically necessary boils down to a subjective preference.[5]

Since, at the same time, we do not have the luxury to fall back, with Leibniz, upon the wisdom of God in order to justify the principle of the identity of indiscernibles as the law governing at least the actually existing order of things[6] we are, once again, forced to confront the issue of particular "bearers" of properties. We have thus come full circle. At the beginning, we have discovered our bearers of properties to be forever elusive and unknowable, and so we opted for the conception of things as bundles of properties. We then found out that this conception must rest upon the principle of the identity of indiscernibles being a necessary truth. No such status, however, could be justifiably attributed to the principle and so we are now once again forced to admit that things do, after all, have something "over and above" their properties—something, that is, by virtue of which even qualitatively indistinguishable things are still numerically different from each other; something that makes each and every thing not simply a collection of properties shared with other things, but also an unique item in the furniture of the world. Up until now, however, we have been unable to encounter any such unique item anywhere.

But perhaps we have not been looking in the right place, talking as we were, all the time, about things like apples and desks and about *their* colors and sizes and shapes. Perhaps something would change were we to shift our attention away from such items and refocus it again upon human beings. And perhaps then some benefit could be derived from our earlier, unsuccessful attempt to abandon contemplation in favor of an active coping with a force standing in our way.

Set up against me in a violent encounter—in a genuine life-and-death struggle—the other's force is indeed a true limit of my powers. As a member of my own species—as a creature endowed with the capacities, the dispositions, and the weapons that are essentially similar to my own—the other turns against me the very same force that I turn against him. His resistance, therefore, is of an entirely different kind than the sort of resistance I have had to confront while attempting to reduce the size of my desk. The encumbering largeness of the desk disappeared quickly in the buzzing of my power saw or under the blows of my axe. Similarly, had I thought that the desk's color did not match the newly repainted walls of my study I would have found no difficulty at all in saturating the desk's surface with a more appropriate color and it might have been *the same* color that I used to paint my kitchen table or my shack. Thus, not only in the attitude of disinterested contemplation but in the very heat of my practical struggles with them, things *are* bundles of properties which I can remove from their original context given the usual, typical means at my disposal. But the other's force bestows upon *his* qualities—both mental and physical—a bond whose strength is in principle beyond the reach of all my means and powers. He matches me tit for tat—in the skill, in the weaponry, in the willingness to go to the brink, and so on. Hence I cannot overcome (or even ignore) the force that pulls together all of his qualities into the unity of *this* particular power center that confronts me. As far as I am concerned, his qualities' bond with each other and with him (their bond with each other on account of their bond with him) is truly unconditioned: were I to try, against his will and given his determination and the means to fight me, to repaint his hair, to shorten his size by a few inches, or to give him an injection to destroy his memories and his mental powers, I would find myself stopped in my tracks. While his hair, his size, and the contents of his mind may still be exactly like the hair, the size, and the mind of, say, his identical twin, they are also unique in that they are bound together in *this* particular power center whose reality I can neither overcome nor ignore. I cannot, that is, decontextualize the other's qualities; here, at long last, I find a force holding them truly together and in one piece. As a force resistant to all my forces, the other imposes himself upon me in the sheer "thisness" of his particularity.

Naturally, to emerge as such a—true and genuine—particular, the other must be endowed with the full wealth of his human qualities: with his muscles and his brain, with his feelings, his thoughts, his actions, and so on. But his having all these qualities, while indeed supplying the necessary condition of his emergence as a particular power center, is not yet sufficient to account for such an emergence. What is still required is that the mere "what" of the other (his qualities) be restructured in a new "how": the other must appear as an adversary in a no-holds-barred violence of the life-and-death struggle. In emerging as such a direct, physical, limit to my powers, the other imposes himself as a genuine particular within my own power stance towards the world—within the very same power stance that modern philosophy, from Hobbes and Descartes on, took up as characteristic of human subjectivity. We need not go beyond that stance and consider the cases of, say, aesthetic or erotic experiences—cases which can be easily analyzed away, given the standpoint of a self bent on achieving control over its environment—in order to discover the ground from which modern philosophy draws its notion of particular bearers of properties.

This unity of a bearer and its properties must not be represented as their external lumping together, which would itself need to be explained. In other words, the other is not an aggregate of two distinct items: of a "bare particular" on the one hand and of a collection of "universal properties" on the other, both of these items mysteriously superimposed upon each other. The other's "thisness" is nothing other than a certain way of organizing his qualities and his relations to his environment: the other emerges as *this* particular power center due to the mobilization of all the determinations that characterize him; without them, he would not be my adversary in a life-and-death struggle, indeed he would be nothing at all. It is for this reason that the particularity of the other ought not to be construed as a distinct item superadded to the collection of universal properties. But neither are we permitted to think of these latter as being *merely* universal and shared by many things. For insofar as a certain group of such properties—the mental and the physical determinations of my adversary in a life-and-death struggle—is fused together in *this* power center that I now confront as the insurpassable limit of my efforts, those properties are all stamped with a unique mark which I can neither erase nor ignore: they are all *his* properties and his alone.

But, one could now justifiably object, normally we attribute particularity not only to persons but to *things* as well; and it now seems as if our earlier (and quite ordinary) talk about *this* apple or *this* desk would have to be considered a sheer mistake or, at best, the result of an unwarranted and animistic projection of our sense of persons onto the world of things. And this cannot be a satisfying conclusion for at least two quite obvious and closely related reasons: first, we do have a strong sense that apples and desks are particulars too and we are not prepared to divest ourselves of that sense which we consider sound and well founded; and, second, the very puzzle we set up at the beginning of the present section was called "the thing and its properties," and it now seems as if we were trying to solve the puzzle by simply ignoring it and shifting the ground of the entire discussion.

But the difficulty brought out by this objection is more apparent than real. While the other as an insurmountable power center in my way is indeed the *original* "this," his presence in the world is tantamount to the (derived, but real) attribution of a similar status to the items functioning as objects of his actual or possible interests. Just as his qualities are beyond my ability to abstract them from their unique bearer—from him—so too are the qualities of, say, his ranch or his cabin. His power flows from him to them: were I to try (against his will and his determination to resist me at any price) to repaint his brown cabin with an outrageous red paint meant to expose him to the neighbors' ridicule, I would soon discover that the ontological integrity of the cabin, its sheer *thisness* that defies my power, is just as real as the original thisness that stands behind it: the force of the other, ready to confront me in a violent encounter.

Imposed upon me by the force of the other, the *conception* of a thing's "thisness" begins to function as part and parcel of a conceptual scheme with the aid of which I understand the world—including all kinds of items which show no connection with other people's interests and desires. But when the background of violence is pushed to the margin, when our sense of it becomes toned down, diluted, or suppressed, things *are* (or are more like) the bundles of properties, since our thought and imagination are then sustained by a practical stance in which the insurmountable *resistance* of the world (of other human agents and, indirectly, of everything else) has been moved from the center to the periphery.

I will conclude this section by touching upon one of those broader issues that are inevitably involved in our decision to accept or reject the principle of the identity of indiscernibles. Leibniz, we remember, grounded the principle in the wisdom of

God as he acts in conformity with the principle of sufficient reason: to create two indiscernible entities would be, Leibniz held, a violation of that fundamental rule guiding the divine choices; in creating two indiscernibles God would be, in effect, acting without reasons. Hence as long as the order of the world remains safely in the hands of a rational and wise God the principle of the identity of indiscernibles must be true.

We may grant this point to Leibniz but, by the same token, we must emphasize its limitations. For if the principle of the identity of indiscernibles—and the bundle-of-properties theory of things which is logically dependent upon it—stands or falls with the belief in the rationality of the world, then it is not surprising that the repudiation of the principle and the vindication of the sheer "thisness" of persons and things goes hand in hand with the discovery of violence—and indeed of *blind violence*[7]—as the harsh and hard limit of reason and of our faith in the power of rationality in general.

II.   Cause and Effect

What has already been said is sufficient to attribute to the other the status of a genuine *causal power*. As my adversary in violence, the other mobilizes a force which I cannot split or divide—a force, we remember, which "holds together" the spatial parts and the qualities it inhabits—and which threatens me with annihilation. There is no escape from such a force. In thus being under the sway of the other's power I am influenced and *affected* by him. Contrary to Hume, then, I *am* acquainted with a causal power. It is simply the power of another human agent viewed as a potential threat to my life in an all-out exchange of violence.

On the other hand, Hume was at least partially right in his repeatedly confessed inability to notice such causal powers. For no causal powers were indeed to be found in the cases—and in the general areas—that he looked over in his search for an impression of such powers. Against Hume—and against Kant as well—it has often been argued[8] that it was a mistake not to have zeroed in on man's strenuous efforts at coping with his physical environment and of thus being exposed to the latter's harsh resistance to human purposes. For through that resistance, some have said and would still say, the world is obviously having an impact upon the human agent; and the agent is thereby given, directly and without any inference, the impression of a causal power that Hume and his followers decreed out of existence. In this quarrel, however, we shall side with Hume. For no causal power can indeed be detected anywhere without taking into account (as neither Hume nor his critics did) that very special center of resistance deployed against me by the other as he is positioning to face me in a life-and-death struggle. This is the only sort of power center that I cannot hold at bay and thus strip it of its entire quality of having an impact upon me. For the very same human powers that allow me to exercise an effective "mastery over nature" remain vulnerable to the powers of another human agent—armed as he is with the capacities, the creativity, and the technology which can always match my own.

In his having an impact upon me—in his emergence as the original causal power—the other injects causal *necessity* into the world. Let us develop this point. The other affects me, but—we recall—he does not affect me as an otherworldly and shadowy creature: the battle that I am about to face will be waged in *this* world of distances, places, tools, physical things, and so on. Were I to sever—even in thought—that connection between the other's menace and the arena of the world, I would be departing from the general facts characterizing the conditions of the human struggle. Now, that connection is nothing else than the connection between the other as the original causal power and the existence of causal necessity in the world. Let us look more carefully. The other is bringing me under the sway of his power: his destructive force, even before it annihilates me in fact, is already envisioned by me as capable of having such an *effect* upon me. Now, for me to perceive the other as capable of such an effect upon me, and for him to be capable of such an effect upon me, the other must be an *effective* causal power: his threat to me must be materialized and embodied in the world. And this truth is not at all the conclusion of my inference from what is immediately and directly given to me in experience. For from the very beginning of the other's emergence as a total and insurmountable threat to me, this threat *is* materialized and embodied in the world: in the stone held by the other's fist, in the sword, in the firing of the gun and the whistling of the

bullet, and so on. Given the conditions of the human struggle—
although, let us repeat again, not apart from and independently
of these conditions—the other cannot have, and cannot be
viewed as having, the causal power vis-à-vis me unless this causal
power of his realizes itself in a chain of events effectively moving
towards my destruction. That chain of events (the armed fist
being raised and falling on my skull, the bullet fired from the
gun and rushing towards my body, the enemy missile exploding
in my town) emerges as a *fate* (a *necessity*) through the very same
stance by which I grasp the other in his capacity of a genuine and
effective causal power. Given the general framework of the
human struggle, these two stances imply each other; indeed
they are the two aspects of one and the same stance toward the
other. For me to have the grasp of the human adversary as the
original causal power is to have the grasp of him as having that
original impact upon me through the world, that is, through a
sequence of events culminating in my destruction. Unless some
such—truly *inevitable and fateful*—sequences of events at the
other's command exist effectively in the world, I must deny the
other his very power to bring about my death. But this I cannot
do except by fantasizing myself out of the human condition.

When I do abstract from my sense of violence and my rooted-
ness in a violent world, causal powers and necessities vanish
from the picture and leave me with mere order and regularity in
the unfolding of events. Nothing more is to be arrived at from
the point of view of an observer detached from the background
of human violence. And nothing more is needed to accommodate the conception of lawfulness as we employ it in scientific
knowledge; such knowledge does not require any talk about
causal powers and necessities. But this is not where those
powers and necessities originate and this is not where they are to
be found. Their persistent reemergence in our conceptual
scheme is due to the experiential context within which man finds
himself prior to and independently of any scientific inquiry: the
context of a violent world. To the extent that this context is
"natural" to man—to the extent that the exposure to violence
must be counted among the general facts of the human condition—the language of causal powers and necessities will resist
all our attempts to replace it with an artificially crippled vocabulary of mere order and regularity and lawfulness.

Since it is the world that supplies the grounding of causal

necessity, the attribution of the latter to connections between objects encountered in the world is not at all due to an animistic and anthropomorphic projection transferring the qualities of human agency onto the items that lack any such qualities to begin with. Just as the emergence of various items around us as the truly "particular" power centers was—as we saw in our earlier section—a real and not an imaginary change in their status, so too is their emergence as vehicles of causal necessity. The other's causal power *is* in the impulse that he gives to a chain of events moving toward my destruction, and these events, therefore, do carry with them the inevitability of my fate. I too am a link in that chain insofar as I am chained to a violent world. This does not imply, needless to say, that my grasp of causal necessity is limited only to the narrow area of events threatening me with destruction. What the claim does imply, however, is that our very conception of events as governed by causal necessity (over and above mere order, regularity, and lawfulness of their appearance) has its ultimate grounding in the experiential context of violence. Since, in both Hume and Kant, that original context of human violence is passed over and ignored, Kant's defense of causal necessity will implicate him in a metaphysics of the transcendental faculties of mind that produce, in a mysterious way, the world of experience. It will be instructive, for our purposes in the present study, to show how Kant's often insightful analyses of causality in the Second Analogy of Experience will not produce the justification of causal necessity unless supplemented with that dubious metaphysics of the transcendental faculties of mind. The problem of causal necessity is genuine and its compelling presence in our modern philosophical problematic is not surprising, as that problematic feeds on man's sense of living and thinking in a violent world. This world is the very birthplace of our ways of philosophizing; and this birthmark is visible not only in the glaring examples of a political philosophy shaped by the heritage of Hobbes and Machiavelli but also in Descartes' "I think therefore I am"—the battle cry against the "evil demon," personifying the hostile forces arrayed against an individual—and in a host of other central philosophical issues, some of which we have had the opportunity to discuss in the first section of the present study. The case of causal necessity is not at all different in this respect.

In a significant passage of the *Critique of Pure Reason* Kant points out exactly what he thinks is wrong with the Humean position: "The concept of cause, for instance, which expresses the necessity of an event under a presupposed condition, would be false if it rested only on an arbitrary subjective necessity, implanted in us, of connecting certain empirical representations according to the rule of causal relation. I would not then be able to say that the effect is connected with the cause *in the object, that is to say, necessarily* . . . " (*CPR*, B168; my emphasis).

This passage will define the line of examination we shall adopt in our analysis of the main body of Kant's argument on causality, put forward in the section on the Second Analogy. Two questions need to be raised and answered. First: why, in what sense, and how successfully can Kant claim that the effect is connected with its cause "in the object"? Second: granted that Kant is successful in the first claim, does it then follow—as Kant thinks it does—that the connection of the cause and the effect "in the object" means their "necessary" connection? It will appear, as we go on, that while the Second Analogy can supply reasons for the first claim, it is on much shakier grounds as far as the second claim is concerned—and yet it is *that* claim which plays the pivotal role in Kant's attempt to justify causal necessity.

Kant's exposition of the Second Analogy may lend itself even more easily to the "patchwork theory" interpretation than the theory's original testing ground—the Transcendental Deduction of the categories. Clearly, in the process of unfolding his main argument on causality Kant pursues different strands of thought which spring up and branch off in surprisingly unpredictable ways. Even more important—and more menacing—is the circumstance that the indispensable premises of the main argument are often supported, or even introduced, at a much later stage of the exposition. The main argument itself is marred with unnecessary repetitions, and Kant's confusing explanations often succeed only in opening up a host of new issues, only remotely related to the problem at hand.

In spite of all this, however—and not unlike in the case of the Transcendental Deduction itself—the Second Analogy does supply one consistent argument about causality. What Kant starts with is our undeniable and all-pervasive awareness of change. We are, to begin with, aware of alterations in our experience: items that we perceive do not remain the same, but undergo modifications in quality; in addition, some such items begin to be while others cease to be, and so on. Now, while our perception of such empirical alterations is indispensable to the emergence of our consciousness of change, this consciousness embraces *all* of our experiences—including those in which no alteration can be detected. Suppose we imagine a fully developed human self confronted with a perceptual field where nothing at all is altering and where all things, with all of their qualities and relations, are frozen, as it were, in one enduring constellation. Even such a self would not lose its awareness of change. For, as Kant explains (*CPR* A199, B245), *every* appearance may be viewed as consequent and following upon something else. Everything, that is (and thus also our frozen perceptual field) may be viewed as taking, or as having taken, place—i.e., as something that happens (*CPR* A198, B243), as an "event" (ibid.). But since we cannot apprehend anything as following upon empty time, every event must be apprehended as following upon another event that took place *before* it (A192, B237). And this is another way of saying that awareness of at least some change cannot be removed from the overall framework of our empirical consciousness.

Our consciousness of being exposed to occurrences of events demands some notion of a temporal chronology. To say that the event *E* happens or takes place is tantamount to the acknowledgment of the requirement of ascribing a date to *E*. A date, in turn, is determinable only within a system of chronological relations of "earlier," "later," etc. While some of these relations may be—provisionally at least—neglected in our assignment of a date to *E*, there is at least one relation that must be taken into account in even the most modest attempt to date events—and that is simply the relation of these events to their (immediate) past: "When . . . I perceive that something happens, this representation first of all contains [the consciousness] that there is something preceding, because only by reference to what precedes does the appearance acquire its time-relation, namely, that of existing after a preceding time in which it itself was not" (*CPR* A198, B243). The task of determining what was happening immediately before *E* took place is thus part and parcel of the task of securing a date for *E* itself.

The securing of the date for an event is a *task* for, in effect, we are here confronted with a difficulty which can only be removed by the application of certain rules and criteria. The difficulty is endemic to our experience as a whole and in every one of its aspects—and hence also to our grasp of temporal succession. For, in general terms, the difference between how things *are* (in a certain respect) and how they *appear* (in the same respect) to this or that subject at this or that stage of his life history is not all given in experience, and yet this very difference is implied in the notion of our having any experience whatever. This difference, therefore, must first be established through a process of ordering and sorting out one's private perceptions by their agreement or disagreement with the public world constructed in conformity with the laws of understanding. The task of establishing this difference must also be faced up to in the case of dating events and placing them within the order of succession: we must have a criterion for discriminating between, on the one hand, what may only appear to be prior in time to our event E and, on the other hand, what truly is prior in time to E. Furthermore, it is the underlying premise of all the three Analogies of Experience that no temporal relation in and between contents of our experience can be established by determining their positions in reference to time itself. For time itself is not an object of my (or anyone else's) possible experience and hence I must have other yardsticks for determining temporal relations. Thus, to establish whether A has indeed occurred prior to B I must be able to order A and B by determining how they stand with respect to each other; and this determination presents a problem, since their objective chronological ordering is not given in my mere representation of them.

The task can at once be rendered more specific as there is one truly important distinguishing mark of an objective succession of events: the irreversibility of the order in which they appear. For if B truly *is* later than A, then B could not have taken place without A already having taken place; while if B only appears to be later than A, then we may well succeed in producing a sequence of representations where B appears prior to the appearance of A. Thus, in Kant's famous examples (*CPR* A190–92; B235–37), when I produce successive perceptions of a large house, the order of succession is purely subjective and I can thus easily reverse my perceptions (I can first focus on the basement and then move my eyes toward the roof; or I can start with the roof and apprehend the lower parts subsequently, etc.); in contrast, when I perceive a ship moving downstream, my perception of the ship's lower position could not have preceded my perception of its higher position—here the order of succession is imposed by the object and thus is truly irreversible.

This irreversible ordering of events is due to nothing other than the operation of causal laws. In effect, if the event E' is to follow upon the event E not simply in our representations of E and E' but in the objective order of the public world, then E must be the condition upon which E' will follow according to a *rule*—for, in Kant's view, it is precisely this rule-like or law-like character of certain representations that allows us to grasp them as expressing the objective order of things. And the rule here required is precisely the rule binding together the sequence of cause and effect (CPR B234). This does not mean that in all cases of establishing the objective chronology of events the succeeding event will actually be caused by the event that took place immediately before it; clearly, and as Kant's critics were quick to point out, the night does follow the day in the objective order of events, and yet no one claims that the day is itself the cause of the night. But this is besides the point. The sequence day-night is an objective one, for the appearance of the night after the day is still due to the operation of causal laws (governing the rotation of the earth on its axis, and so on).

But what, exactly, has Kant proved to us so far? His first impulse is to tell us point-blank that he has just presented us with a proof of causal *necessity*. He insists on this word again and again: "But in the perception of an event there is always a rule that makes the order in which the perceptions (in the apprehension of this appearance) follow upon one another a *necessary* order" (CPR, A193–B238); an event must be referred to "something else which precedes it and upon which it follows in conformity with a rule, *that is, of necessity* (CPR, A194–B239; my emphasis). Kant concludes this part of his defense of causal necessity with a statement—"the experience of an event (i.e., of anything as *happening*) is itself possible only on this assumption" (CPR A195–B240)—which he immediately interprets as a direct refutation of Hume:

This may seem to contradict all that has hitherto been taught in regard to the procedure of our understanding. The accepted view is that only through the perception and comparison of events repeatedly following in a uniform manner upon preceding appearances we are enabled to discover a rule according to which certain events always follow upon certain appearances, and that is the way in which we are first led to construct for ourselves the concept of cause. Now, the concept, if thus formed, would be merely empirical, and the rule which it supplies, that everything which happens has a cause, would be as contingent as the experience upon which it is based. (*CPR* A196–B241)

I have quoted this passage at full length, for it will lead us to the very core of Kant's entire argument. For let us grant that (a) the conception and the determination of the objective succession of events is indispensable to our having any experience whatever and that (b) such conception and determination of the objective succession implies the use of causal laws governing the changing world. But do these two claims, even if sound, add up to produce—against Hume—a justification of causal necessity?

Clearly, in the examples given—the ship moving downstream, the stove heating the room (*CPR* A202–B248), etc.—the causal laws that we employ as marks of objective succession are entirely empirical and discovered by experience. If, therefore, *they* are quite sufficient to mark off the objective from the subjective succession, then this function of causality need not imply any necessity in the connection between the cause and the effect. The necessity of there being some causal laws in no way warrants Kant's (further) claim to the effect that these causal laws must also reflect a necessity in the connection of causes and effects. This last claim does not follow from the argument of the Second Analogy and is entirely unnecessary to defend the soundness of claims (a) and (b).

As a matter of fact Kant himself seems to be aware of that gap in the argument. For immediately after staking out his big claim against (Hume's) "accepted view" that causal laws are only our generalizations of empirical regularities, he begins to feel the need to give his claim an additional support:

We have, then, to show, in the case under consideration that we never, *even in experience,* ascribe succession (that is, the happening of some event which previously did not exist) to the object, and so distinguish it from subjective sequence in our apprehension, except when there is an underlying rule which compels us to observe this order of perceptions rather than any other; nay, that this compulsion is really what first makes possible the representation of a succession in the object. (*CPR*, A196, B241; my emphasis)

But the restatement of the proof that now follows is still insufficient to show that "even in experience" we ascribe objective succession to events only on the requirement of a (strong and non-Humean) causal *necessity* in their relation. What Kant does show—again—is merely that our ascription of objective succession implies the existence of some law-like regularities in the appearance of succeeding events; but this is still a far cry from the justification of his attribution of a (strong and not merely empirical) necessity to those regularities.

How does Kant try to show that "even in experience" our sorting out of objective from subjective succession implies causal necessity? He begins by drawing the distinction between the subjective and the objective "meaning" (*Bedeutung*) of our representations. The objective meaning of our representations is simply their reference beyond the realm of our private mental states and toward the object of experience. But, Kant contends, such objective meaning cannot be attributed to certain of our representations by matching them against some (very special) representation of the object itself. For then *that* representation, in turn—and simply on account of its being also a representation—would have to be certified in its pretension to have the objective meaning that it claims to have, and so on. Since nothing but representations are given to us, the objective meaning of this or that representation can be attributed to it only due to its conformity with a certain type of immanent criterion. The difference between the subjective and the objective meaning boils down to the absence or presence of a *rule,* and so Kant concludes that the representations' "*relation to an object*" (*CPR* A197, B242) "results only in subjecting the representations to a rule" (ibid). Kant goes on to identify the rule—of causality—needed to secure the objective meaning for our representations of succession, and he then asserts that the (just demonstrated) existence of causal connections between events has "a twofold consequence. In the first place, I cannot reverse the series, placing that which happens prior to that upon which it follows. And secondly, if the state which precedes is posited, this determinate event follows *inevitably and necessarily*" (*CPR* A198, B244; my emphasis).

However, even if we are now warranted in positing an irreversible sequence of phenomena, thanks to our employment of causal laws, and even if such employment of causal laws is indeed necessary for there to be any experience, it still does not follow that these causal laws must reflect some "inevitability" or "necessity" binding effects to their causes. For all we know, these laws could very well express nothing more than ordered regularities in the appearance of events and could still do the job of separating subjective from objective successions.

A Kantian's reply to this line of criticism is easy to anticipate. It is not, he will say, the (inevitably empirical) *content* of causal laws that is to be thought of as reflecting the necessity of the cause-effect connection, but the mere *form* of the law, i.e., the general status of lawfulness as such. Now this is undoubtedly the correct answer, but it is also largely irrelevant to the issue at hand. For we do not discriminate on the grounds of lawfulness as such between subjective and objective perceptions of, say, the chronological positions of fire and smoke in relation to each other but on the grounds of a specific law with a specific content. At the very best, then, Kant could claim that the element of necessity is *thought into* the particular causal laws due to their subjection to the form of lawfulness in general. As for the connection between necessity and the form of lawfulness in general, the proof of such a connection—implied, Kant argues, by the transcendental unity of apperception—can be found in the Transcendental Deduction.

Once again, the reply is correct and well taken, but let us grasp clearly its implications for the issue of causal necessity. It now turns out that the reason why Kant deemed it justifiable to impute his "inevitability" and "necessity" to the cause-effect relation had little to do with the requirement of discriminating between objective and subjective chronology of events and much to do with Kant's own doctrines from the Transcendental Deduction. And this has two highly undesirable consequences: (a) we are unable to justify causal necessity *in its own terms* and (b) in order to accept Kant's justification of causal necessity we must be prepared to buy—lock, stock, and barrel—Kant's entire picture of our mind as somehow "producing" the world of experience (and thus endowing it with necessary connections) through the exercise of the transcendental faculties of synthesis. We would be much better off, it seems, if we could avoid paying the price of (a) or of (b)—or, preferably, of both—for saving causal necessity.

There seem to be, however, some still other and still different trends of thought in the section on the Second Analogy. In what Kemp Smith, for instance, considers to be Kant's *fourth* proof of causality[9] Kant attempts to account for the necessity of the cause-effect sequence by grounding it in the very nature of time. The point was already hinted at earlier (*CPR*, A194–B239)—and this fact alone is sufficient to disprove the claim that we are given here an entirely new proof—but, for some reason, it is only at the present stage of his analysis (*CPR*, A199–B244) that Kant decides to bring it to the fore of his argument. The main idea seems clear and simple enough: since in time itself any instant (say t') cannot but succeed the instant preceding it (say t), and since all events take place in time, it follows that what takes place in t' (say E') must inevitably come after what takes place in t (say E). Thus the "necessity" implied in the causal connection between E and E' does not come from the mere form of lawfulness in general—much less from the specific content of this or that particular law—but from the subjection of events to the form of time. Since every part of time is necessarily dependent in its occurrence upon the preceding part of time having already taken place, the same necessary dependence is carried over to the events occurring *in* these parts of time.

But Kant's own formulation of his new point allows us to see immediately the return of the old difficulty:

> If, then, it is a necessary law of our sensibility, and therefore a *formal condition* of all perceptions, that the preceding time necessarily determines the succeeding (since I cannot advance to the succeeding time save through the preceding), it is also an indispensable law of *empirical representation* of the time-series that the appearances of past time determine all existences in the succeeding time, and that these latter, as events, can take place only in so far as the appearances of past time determine their existence in time, that is, determine them according to a rule. (*CPR* A199, B244)

Now there are two distinct and independent claims put forward in this passage. It is one thing to claim—appealing to the "necessary law of our sensibility"—that parts of time itself are arranged in an irreversible order and that therefore t' (and thus also E') can only take place if t (and thus also E) has already taken place. It is quite another thing to say—as Kant just said again—that the dependence of E' upon E is due to a *rule*. We can easily imagine how the second claim could be false even if the first claim were to be true. Suppose we want to make an experiment by watching Kant's ship as it moves downstream. On the first day of the experiment the ship is upstream at 8 A.M. and downstream at 9 A.M. On the second day, however, the ship is downstream at 8 A.M. and upstream at 9 A.M. On the third day the sequence noticed on the first day returns again; then—for a change—we have a couple of days with a sequence noticed on the second day, etc. At every one of these days the *time t'* (9 A.M.) inevitably and invariably follows the *time t* (8 A.M.). But there are no rules or even regularities governing the appearances of *events*. The necessary dependence of the occurrence of t' upon the prior occurrence of t (where both t and t' are taken merely as parts of time itself) is perfectly compatible with a total randomness in the occurrence of events taking place *in t* and t'.

It will of course be replied, by a Kantian, that such an odd universe would be incompatible with the requirement of an unified experience (including the experience of the very difference between 8 A.M. and 9 A.M.) and— ultimately—with the requirement of a unified self. In fact, Kant himself immediately points out (*CPR,* A200, B245) that the need for a "rule" is implied by our inability to have the experience of time itself and thus also by our inability to establish the chronology of events through their reference to time itself. All of this has been argued before. Precisely for this reason, however, the old difficulty reappears. Again: even if we grant Kant that there necessarily must be *some* rules governing the occurrence of events it does not yet follow that these rules must express some nonempirical necessity (and not simply the observed uniformities and regularities) binding the chains of events. Such kind of necessity is implied *neither* by the notion of t' necessarily following upon t, *nor* by the need of there being some rules governing the succession of events taking place in, respectively, t and t'. To return to our earlier conclusion: if there is to be causal necessity in our world, it must originate entirely in the transcendental mental activities responsible for the production of that world as a whole. Nothing short of that move will vindicate causal necessity.[10] But that move, we remember, does not allow us to defend causal necessity on the merits of the causal necessity's own case; and, in addition, the move sends us back to the undesired embraces of Kant's idealistic metaphysics of transcendental faculties of mind.

We have, at the beginning of this section and following upon our earlier analyses, searched elsewhere for the origin and the foundation of causal necessity. We have searched for them in the experiential context of man's standing in the human world—and that means also in the world of human violence. It is here that the notion of causal necessity finds its ultimate grounding. For due to the violence that other humans unleash, or threaten to unleash against me, the mere regularities and uniformities in my environment gain the additional quality of *inevitability and fate*. The other—and he alone—can impose this quality both upon me and upon the sequences of events I must concern myself with. Conversely, when I abstract from the experiential context of violence, causal necessity vanishes without a trace, leaving me with mere regularity and uniformity in the unfolding of events.

And the same fate—and for the same reason—befalls my conception of causal *power*. On this point too the failure of Kant's attempt to correct Hume is quite instructive. To be sure, compared to the attention Kant has lavished upon causal necessity, the treatment of causal power in the Second Analogy enjoys only a marginal place. This is quite understandable, as Kant was everywhere concerned, above all, with justifying certain necessary laws underlying the possibility of experience. Nevertheless, Kant fully realized that our talk about causation covers more than simply the law-like necessity in the appearance and disappearance of events. The *dynamical* aspect of causation, Kant knew, had to be given its due. He was so strongly convinced of this aspect's paramount importance to our notion of causality, that the first and the original title he gave to the principle he argued for in the Second Analogy was the Principle of Production (*CPR*, A189). And if, in the second edition of the

Critique, Kant decided to drop his initial reference to an
Erzeugung from the title of the Second Analogy, he had by no
means abandoned his commitment to the view of causes as
powers. Immediately after the presentation of his main argument in favor of the causal principle he informs his readers that
"causality leads to the concept of action, this in turn to the
concept of force, and thereby to the concept of substance"
(*CPR,* A204, B249). Kant is quite clear that the implied connection between all of these notions—of cause, action, force,
and substance—is entirely conceptual and, therefore, requires
no other justification than our mere analysis of them (ibid.).
Any attempt to consider *A* as a cause but not as a force is thus to
be rejected on the grounds of logic alone; our description of *A* as
the cause of *B* cannot be logically independent of our description of *A* as a force or power having an influence over *B*.

But Kant's *claim* to this effect—the claim that we must separate from his claims about causal necessity—remains unsupported by the argument deployed in the Second Analogy. In fact,
even if one were prepared to grant Kant that he *had* succeeded in
proving the existence of some necessary laws governing the
succession of effects upon their causes, one would still find no
support in that proof for Kant's further claims concerning the
dynamical quality of causes. If causes are to be viewed as forces,
we need to be convinced of this by some additional considerations. And our very need for such additional considerations casts
a shadow upon Kant's entire claim that the connection between
the notions of cause and force is indeed of a merely conceptual
nature. For throughout his main argument Kant has been relying
upon a concept of cause, and he has been putting that concept to
numerous uses, without being in the slightest compelled to
construe it as logically implying the concept of force. The concept
of cause as mere conformity to a law—even to a necessary law—
in the sequence of events was employed as entirely independent
of the concept of cause as force, power, etc.

It is for these reasons, one may presume, that Kant felt he
owed his readers some additional explanation of that postulated
connection between the concepts at issue. But the explanation
he went on to offer creates even more confusion. In effect, Kant
is not even sure as to what kind of explanation is needed here.
On the one hand, he asserts that the explanation called for does

not belong to the *Critique of Pure Reason* but to the "future system of pure reason" (*CPR* A202, B249); for, he points out (ibid.), the *Critique of Pure Reason* is concerned only with justifying our synthetic a priori knowledge, while the issue at hand is a subject for a mere analysis of concepts. Were we to follow this suggestion we would have to wait for and depend upon Kant's analysis in the *Metaphysical Foundations of Natural Science* (1786), where the concept of force is indeed found to be implied by the concept of matter and hence also, *eo ipso*, by the concept of a material object qua cause. But Kant himself is dissatisfied with this suggestion, for immediately after conveying it to us he hastens to tell himself: "But I must not leave unconsidered the empirical criterion of substance, in so far as substance appears to manifest itself not through permanence of appearance, but more adequately and easily through action" (*CPR*, A204, B249). It is plain that Kant is here on sound grounds in repudiating his first, cavalier, suggestion—or at least in qualifying it so severely as to blunt entirely its cutting edge. For if the notion of cause is indeed conceptually connected with the notions of force, action, and substance insofar as the latter "appears to manifest itself . . . through action," then we cannot wait for Kant's analysis of the (much more specific) concept of matter in order to discover the connection we have missed thus far. As Kant is now fully aware, the connection should be made clear in terms of such uses of the notion of cause—applicable, according to Kant, to psychological causation as well—as we have encountered within the main argument of the Second Analogy.

Kant, however, fails to clarify this connection. The answer he gives (*CPR* A205, B250) may be interpreted in two ways.[11] The dynamical and truly active aspect of causation may first be looked for in the *noumenal* counterparts of what we take to be empirically observable causes. Thus while the mere need to establish the objective chronology of events requires no more than the conception of causes as phenomena lawfully conjoined with their effects, causes are also vehicles of powers insofar as we construe them as having a noumenal side to them. However (and apart from the usual difficulties involved in any talk about noumena), this solution is in flagrant contradiction with Kant's present purposes and with his own, quite unambiguously stated, description of these purposes. For Kant is—as he must be—fully committed to the ascription of a power to the cause viewed as "substance (as phenomenon)" (ibid.); it is by analyzing precisely such a "concept of a substance as appearance" (*CPR* A206, B251) that we must be able to discover the dynamical quality of causes. No such analysis, however, is actually produced by Kant as he proceeds to offer the explanation we have been waiting for all along. He simply, and arbitrarily, stipulates that "Action *signifies* the relation of the subject of causality to its effect" (ibid.; my emphasis).

In the light of our earlier considerations, however, this connection between the concepts of cause, power, and substance ceases to be baffling. The original substances in our world—the original bearers of properties and parts—are nothing other than the very same human centers of force that we have also discovered to be the loci of causal powers. All of these concepts, while not empirical, are applicable to the empirical world—they need not and do not refer us to the mysterious *Jenseits* of noumena—and all of them belong to one and the same family of concepts; thus the concept of the other as a force fusing together its qualities and its parts (the concept of substance, that is) implies the concept of the other as the causal power having an inevitable impact upon me (and vice versa: the concept of the other as a causal power implies the concept of the other as substance). Given the experiential context of human violence, the connection between all those concepts (of cause and power and force and substance) can indeed be discovered by analysis; but this is also another way of saying that the analysis in question is parasitic upon our sense of participating in a violent world.

III.   Freedom and Origination

The results of the preceding section can be put in quite traditional terms. The existence of causal necessity in the world finds its condition of possibility in the menacing presence of the other. And in his capacity as the condition of possibility of causal necessity in the world the other emerges as characterized by a number of features we have not yet had the opportunity to focus on.

In the first place, the capacity to start a causal chain is not attributed to the other because of an arbitrary selection of one particular item from a larger set of conditions (events, processes, etc.). The raging snowstorm I now watch through the window may well be considered as the effect of either those dark clouds covering the sky, or of the low-pressure system moving in on the mountains from the Pacific, or of certain atmospheric conditions which created that low-pressure system somewhere near the Hawaiian Islands; but when the other affects me by his threat, this threat is due to *him*. To be sure—as we noted so many times—the threat is unfolded and deployed in the world and in the sequences of worldly events: in the barrel of a rifle aimed at me, in the open space between myself and the other, in the bullet's being fired and moving toward me, and so on. But it is the other—and he *alone*—who stands out as the source of a series of events moving toward my destruction. In his capacity as the original causal power, the other stands out as a truly particular and discrete "this"; and so that fateful chain of events issues from him as a power center set apart from everything around and outside him. It is not some continuous and complex "state of affairs" or a whole "state of the universe" which causes the threat to unfold: it is him.

In the second place—and paradoxically—insofar as the other is the original causal power injecting causal necessity into the world, he himself emerges as *free*. And so not only must the causal necessity yield a substantive chunk of its territory to the rule of freedom, but, in point of fact, there would be no causal necessity at all if human freedom did not exist and did not operate effectively in the very same world where causal necessity is to be found.

The reader will pardon me if I now summarize and build upon an argument I have offered elsewhere.[12]

I am subject to causal necessity insofar as I am powerless toward, and powerless to escape from, the threat represented by the other. But to represent such a—total and insurmountable—threat, the other must be threatening me as a free agent. In effect, if the threat is due not to a free activity but to a brute and merely given event, then the threat itself can be neutralized; I can always hope to control it, to escape it, to ignore it; whereas the threat imposing upon me subjection to causal necessity does not leave me with any possibility of holding it at bay. Let us look more carefully at this difference between the threat of *events* and the threat of *free actions*. Due to the creativity and inventiveness of the other, his threat can never be put behind me. He can always threaten me with a new technology or a new course of action for which I am not prepared. Furthermore, since the presence of the other is not confined to a particular area—since I live in a human *world*—the threat represented by his creativity is not simply local and parochial (thus some unpredictable, perhaps even uncaused event taking place here and now), but general and all-pervasive. And only due to this general and all-pervasive creativity of the other his threat is in principle beyond my powers (as the threat of an unpredictable or even uncaused event is not, at least as long as we concern ourselves with the concrete possibilities confronting man in his life-world and not with some abstract and far-fetched scenarios). Insofar, then, as the other is willing to forgo all the inducements I may use—all the means of persuasion and pressure at my disposal—to tie him down and to control him, and insofar as he exercises his creativity, he endangers the foundation of my being. It is as a creative force deployed over against me that the other imposes upon me subjection to the iron grip of causal necessity.

In the third place—and this follows from what was said above—the other imposes upon me the idea of a power of *originating* new causal chains. For the novelty and the unexpectedness of a mere event—as well as the issuing novelty and unexpectedness of its consequences—can be coped with, given our established technologies and skills. The shock waves of an event can thus be absorbed by my past, by what I take for granted. Only the other's shock may not be so absorbed due to his purposeful acts of creativity (his truly free acts), thanks to which he is incessantly coming up with ever new skills and technologies and taking new and innovative courses of action.

The themes we have outlined above—the themes of freedom, of its existence in the world, of its power to originate new sequences of events—must be counted as belonging to the very core of the modern philosophical problematic. Our approach to these themes must now be tested by a closer analysis and by a confrontation with the way in which they have been articulated in philosophical discussions. Once again, the theory of Kant will serve as the testing ground of our approach. For in Kant's treatment of freedom the themes we have just explored have been brought together in a theory meant to incorporate and to do justice to the main rival accounts put forward in the golden age of modern philosophy. If we can show—as we intend to—that Kant's claims and solutions are either unsupported or incoherent, and that these shortcomings disappear when the analysis of freedom is conducted from within the experiential context of human violence, we will have succeeded in showing that that context is indeed at the root of the entire problematic of freedom. It was the great merit of Hegel to have recognized that experiential context of violence as the condition of human freedom, even though—as we may add in anticipation of our analyses in the next chapter—Hegel's rationalistic and idealistic biases proved to be a powerful distorting influence upon his attempts to come to terms with the notion of violence.

Let us now turn to Kant's treatment of freedom in his explanation of and solution to the Third Antinomy of Pure Reason. When the principle of causality is cast as an unconditioned rule embracing the totality of what exists—that is, the totality of things as they are independently of our actual or possible experience of them—the principle yields two incompatible propositions. The first proposition (the thesis) affirms, while the second (the antithesis) denies, the existence of freedom in the world. The proofs of these two conflicting propositions unfold the implications of what I will call, with A. C. Ewing, the "two different aspects"[13] of the causal principle construed as an unconditioned law of the order of things. This description of what takes place in the Third Antinomy is carefully chosen. On the one hand, both the thesis and the antithesis are demonstrable on the same grounds—on the grounds of our (unwarranted) ascription of causal necessity to the order of things. This is implied by Kant's overall strategy in the Antinomies: an antinomy is genuine only if it starts with one conception and, by exploring *its* implications, produces two valid proofs of two incompatible propositions. Only due to that circumstance can we diagnose the underlying conception as being in some sense inherently flawed or at least misapplied. On the other hand, however, both the thesis and the antithesis must be viewed as exploring two different—albeit equally necessary—aspects of the underlying conception. For if—to shift back to the case of the Third Anti-

nomy—the proofs of both the thesis and the antithesis pro-
ceeded from one and the same aspect of the causal principle,
then they could contradict each other only in the sense that one
of these proofs would be valid while the other was faulty; but
then there would be no antinomy generated by the principle of
causality.

With these preliminary comments in mind we can now spell
out the conflict brought out in the Third Antinomy.

The antinomy's thesis is an affirmation of freedom in the
world: "Causality in accordance with laws of nature is not the
only causality from which the appearances of the world can one
and all be derived. To explain these appearances it is necessary to
assume that there is also another causality, that of freedom"
(*CPR* A444, B472).

The supporting argument which follows immediately is
composed of a number of important points.

We take for granted—and the Second Analogy proves us
right in this respect—that every event must have a cause. What
about the latter, though? Does the cause of an event demand its
own cause? It seems clear that it does, for every cause in nature
must itself be an *event* or "something which has taken place"
(ibid.), and all events must have causes. But why, exactly, must
the cause of an event be itself an event? Because, Kant argues, on
the contrary supposition we could not even account for our
initial event being an "event," i.e., something that "occurs" and
"takes place." In effect, all such and similar expressions imply
the reference to time: when we say that an event takes place we
mean that the event happens at a certain moment of *time*. But,
Kant goes on (ibid.), if the cause of the "event were to have been
some preceding state" which "had always existed," then the
event itself as that cause's "consequence also would have always
existed, and would not have only just arisen" (ibid.). And this is
another way of saying that the alleged "event" would not have
been an event at all. In effect, there are only two possibilities
open here. Either *A is* the cause of *B* and so whenever there is *A*,
B must follow suit—and thus if *A* had "always" existed, *B* would
have to have existed in an equally permanent fashion, and hence
not as an event. Or if *A* occurs without necessitating the occurrence of *B*, then *A* is not truly the cause of *B*, and something
else—a *C* or a *D*—must be posited as responsible for *B*'s occur-

rence. But in this case it would be necessary for C or D to be an event (and not something that had "always existed"), for otherwise B itself "would have always existed" instead of beginning to exist at a particular and identifiable moment of time. And so, Kant concludes, all causes of events are themselves events; qua events they, in turn, demand their own causes.

All of the above was implied by the "law of nature" (ibid.)—that is, by unconditioned determinism—and it is also on the grounds of this "law of nature" that the thesis takes its next step. Since "this law of nature is just this, that nothing takes place without a cause sufficiently determined *a priori*" (*CPR* A446, B474), it will appear—we shall soon see how—that determinism, "when taken in unlimited universality" will prove to be "self-contradictory" (ibid.) as it will imply its own denial in affirming the existence of freedom.

But Kant's very first move in that direction is fraught with dangers and full of ambiguities. Clearly, when he says that the "law of nature" implies—indeed it "is just this," as he just put it—that "nothing takes place without a cause, sufficiently determined *a priori*" (*hinreichend a priori bestimmte Ursache*) he does not refer merely to the various requirements of our ordinary causal explanations. Already Schopenhauer has seen[14] that Kant's sweeping statement is entirely unneeded to meet the requirements of our causal explanations: When I say that A is the cause of B, all I need to know is whether the occurrence of A is sufficient to account for the occurrence of B; I do not need to inquire into the (further and independent) question about the cause of A itself. If, then, Kant's "sufficiently determined cause" of B were to be equivalent with B's "sufficient cause," Kant would have no right to claim that our search for causes be extended over A itself.

And yet if our ordinary causal explanations do not demand such a search, something else does. Determinism leads us into contradiction insofar as it claims that "nothing" takes place without a "sufficiently determined cause." What yields the contradiction is not the principle of causality itself but our conception of it as the unconditioned law governing the independent order of things. In effect, Kant goes on to argue, "If . . . everything takes place solely in accordance with laws of nature, there will always be only a relative and never a first

beginning, and consequently no completeness of the series on
the side of the causes that arise the one from the other" (ibid.).
The key demand for a "completeness" on the side of the causes
is; again, incomprehensible otherwise than on the grounds of
the (metaphysical) interpretation given here to the causal principle. Due to that interpretation of the principle, every cause must
itself be sufficiently determined, for in all dialectical (i.e., anti-
nomy-generating) arguments of metaphysicians the major
premise is always: "If the conditioned is given, the entire series
of all its conditions is likewise given" (*CPR* A497, B525). It
follows, furthermore, that we must affirm the existence of a *self-*
caused cause since no cause having a cause other than itself can
meet that requirement of "completeness of the series on the side
of the causes." Now such a self-caused cause, capable of originating new series of events, can be found nowhere else but in an
act of spontaneity and freedom (*CPR* A446, B474). The principle of causality, therefore, when taken in its metaphysical claim
(i.e., as unconditioned determinism) abolishes itself, for it implies consequences—the existence and the causality of freedom—which cannot be true if the principle is to preserve its
unconditioned hold upon the order of things.

It is still the same metaphysical hypostasis of the causal principle that yields both the proof and the proposition of the
antithesis. In effect, an "absolute beginning" of a series of
events—the sort of beginning we have just been led to infer in
the thesis—demands, qua beginning, that it too be preceded by
a cause according to a rule. The thesis's demand for a "sufficiently determined cause" was the first aspect of our conception
of the principle of causality; the antithesis's present demand
represents the (equally important) second aspect of the same
conception. In effect, if we say that something "begins to be,"
we imply that it happens at a certain time; but as everything that
takes place in time must have a cause, we cannot be satisfied with
an occurrence which is not caused by what took place before it.
Yet such would have to be the status of a free act— of "the very
determination . . . of spontaneity to originate a series" (*CPR*
A445, B473)— vis-à-vis anything and everything that took
place before it: "a *dynamical* beginning of the action, if it is also a
first beginning presupposes a state which has no *causal* connection with the preceding state of the cause, that is to say in

nowise follows from it" (ibid.). In other words, while a free act does indeed issue from the agent, it does not issue from whatever it is that the agent was or might have been prior to the performance of that act. And that means that the agent's free performance represents a break in the causal chains and is incompatible with the principle of causality. For this reason— Kant continues in the antithesis—the affirmation of freedom in the world "renders all unity of experience impossible" and must therefore be considered as "an empty thought-entity" (*CPR* A447, B475). Determinism has won.

A number of questions arise immediately and cry out for answers as we ponder the Third Antinomy. I will first mention—and deal with—two obvious questions of particular importance both to the assessment of the argument deployed in the Third Antinomy and to my own approach to the issue of freedom and necessity.

The first question—an objection against the whole edifice built in the thesis—is raised by the "empiricist" spokesman for the antithesis in the Observation on the Third Antinomy. On what grounds—the "empiricist" asks his "dogmatic" opponent—are we to believe that the inferred first cause of events is something more than a mere "resting place for your imagination" (*CPR* A449, B477) invented under the pressure of your inability to conceive an infinite series of causes and effects? Such an infinite series of events would indeed be an "enigma in nature" (ibid.), but we have no right to rule it out.[15]

The second question has more to do with the very concept of freedom employed in the thesis—and it is the same concept that Kant himself will employ, later on, in his own solution of the Third Antinomy. For, Kant will argue, this concept, when stripped of its cognitive pretensions and given a merely "problematic" status—the status of a concept referring, without any truth claim, to what might be the case in the noumenal sphere, i.e., beyond the realm of possible experience—allows us to reconcile freedom and necessity. Now, the concept of freedom put forward and argued for in the thesis has two key components. The first cause of a new series of events has the power to *begin* (or *originate*) that series and, in addition, of doing this *freely* (or *spontaneously*). Why, we may ask Kant, are these two components—of origination and freedom—welded together?

We shall first address the second question for, as we shall see, the answer to it will also allow us to supply the answer to the first question as well. The answers, we may tell the reader beforehand, cannot be found in Kant himself. They can only be found, we may add, when the concept of freedom—the very same concept of freedom that is at the foundation of Kant's own theory—is considered as reflecting our familiarity with the all-pervasive context of a violent world.

In his Observation on the thesis of the Third Antinomy—and throughout the later stages of his argument as well—Kant shows no doubt or second thoughts about conflating the idea of *origination* (of a series of events) with the idea of *freedom* (or spontaneity). In the very opening passage of the Observation on the thesis Kant talks about "The necessity of a first beginning, due to freedom, of a series of appearances" (*CPR* A448, B476). Yet these two ideas are logically independent. Why, one may ask, couldn't we suppose that (brute and unintelligible) *events* are just as capable of originating a new series of events as (free and spontaneous) *actions*? It is not enough to suggest quickly—as Kant does at the very beginning of the Observation on the thesis (ibid.)—that only an action can be "imputable" to the first cause of a chain of events. For if we mean by this that only then can the first cause be held accountable (responsible, blamed, praised, etc.) for its doings, we give no grounds, so far, why the first cause of a chain of events *ought* to be held accountable for originating that chain of events. But if by "imputation" we mean only that the origination of the chain Y is to be ascribed to the item X, then there is no reason at all why X could not be a brute event just as well as it could be a free action.

The overall thrust of Kant's reply to those obvious questions is well known. He first calls upon the distinction between the phenomenal and the noumenal spheres. He then insists—falling back upon his argument from the Second Analogy—that in the phenomenal sphere both events *and* actions are equally subject to the principle of causality. However, he goes on, qua noumenal, actions—and actions alone—escape the grip of causal necessity.

In what follows we shall study in some detail the reasons supporting Kant's position as outlined above. But we can already point out what seems to be—and what will effectively turn out to be—the weak point in his entire construction. Since we cannot know the noumenal sphere anyway, there is no reason why in that sphere all sorts of things might not be possible that are not possible in the phenomenal sphere. And so, when taken in reference to the noumenal sphere, our talk about *events* originating new series of events may not be any less intelligible or less justified than our talk about (free) *actions* originating such series. Were this to turn out to be the case, however, then Kant's conflation of the idea of origination of a series of events with the ideas of freedom and spontaneity would prove to be groundless. Clearly, Kant is under an obligation to convince us that what he regards as the sources of new series of events can only be free and spontaneous actions—and not unintelligible, brute events.

How does Kant try to convince us of the soundness of this crucial claim of his? Let us note immediately that he does not rely upon our ordinary, empirical notions of actions and events—the notions which apply to the world of phenomena. Taken in this empirical sense, actions are just as causally determined as are events. And the causality's grip upon actions is due to the very same circumstance as its grip upon events: regarded as empirical, our actions occur in time and must therefore be viewed (given the argument from the Second Analogy) as effects necessarily following their causes. From this point of view, the very difference between actions and events becomes irrelevant and can be disregarded: "Every action [viewed] as appearance, in so far as it gives rise to an event, *is itself an event* or happening, and presupposes another state wherein its cause is to be found" (*CPR* A543, B571; my emphasis). But this also allows us to sharpen the focus of our initial question. For if actions, no less than ordinary events, are subject to the grip of causal necessity when taken as occurring in the phenomenal world, then on what grounds can Kant claim that actions *alone* can escape that necessity in the noumenal sphere? Why, if their phenomenal status vis-à-vis causal necessity is identical, is their noumenal status so profoundly different in precisely the same respect?

It often looks as if Kant has simply and arbitrarily stipulated restricting the usage of the term "event" to the phenomenal sphere alone. In the treatment of the Third Antinomy Kant takes over the vocabulary he has already familiarized us with in the Second Analogy: an event is a "happening," an "occurrence," or something that "takes place" or "comes to be," etc.— and all such expressions are shot through with reference to time and hence also to the reign of causal necessity. For this reason there can be no uncaused events: "the causality of the cause, which *itself happens* or comes to be, must itself in turn have a cause" (*CPR* A533, B561). There are numerous passages where Kant belabors this point, casting it in ever new terms. It then follows—since only uncaused events could originate new series of events—that no event can originate a new series of events. So far, however, we have not been given anything more than a mere stipulation. The arbitrariness of this stipulation stands out. For if—as Kant has just told us himself—empirically viewed actions are events too but can nonetheless be construed as being beyond the grip of causal necessity in the noumenal sphere, then on what grounds are we to deny that privilege to the entire class of events—be they actions or not? Clearly, there must be something special about human actions which gives them the privilege of enjoying (noumenal) liberation from the tyranny of causal necessity. So far, however, this special element has not been brought out by Kant.

What we are looking for is the reason why the origination of new series of events should be ascribed to free and spontaneous actions of the agent rather than to mere events (occurring outside or inside the agent). What Kant needs is an argument—and not simply an arbitrary stipulation—as to why actions can and events cannot be construed as taking place outside of the phenomenal, temporal world and hence also outside of the area governed by causal necessity. At times, when Kant probes the issue deeper, he suggests that the required difference is due precisely to the *active,* performative feature of the action: "No action begins *in* this active being itself; but we may yet quite correctly say that the active being of *itself* begins its effects in the sensible world" (*CPR* A541, B569). As the agent's own performance, we may say, the action is intelligible in itself—that is, it does not demand from us any search for its causes. For example, my action of chopping wood for the winter is intelligible as it is both to myself and to the neighbors who watch me performing it. We do not need, Kant seems to be saying, to go outside of the action and to search for its causes. In contrast, when the roof in my house collapses suddenly I find it only natural to look for the cause of that collapse. Now, while there may be some things that, as Kant put it, "begin *in*" the agent himself, such things are not the agent's actions, but are also events in spite of the fact that they take place *within* him. For all such things—a sudden mood that comes over me, a brain disturbance I am struck with, etc.— a causal explanation is required. But such things happen *to* the agent; they are not performances of the agent himself. In the cases of the agent's own performance the action's sufficient explanation is to be found in the agent's performance of that action.

But this cannot be the *differentia specifica* we have been expecting. The only difference between actions and events we have been shown so far was found entirely within the ordinary, empirical sphere; this difference is embedded in our ordinary, empirical understanding of actions and events. Clearly, I do not find the action of chopping wood immediately intelligible to me because I view it as occurring outside of time, within the noumenal realm. Moreover, according to Kant, this direct intelligibility of an action is in any case quite superficial if not altogether apparent. For all empirical actions (and hence also my action of chopping wood) are, in the last analysis, unintelligible without being traced back to their causes, so much so that the very difference between (empirical) actions and events comes close to vanishing altogether (*CPR* A543, B571). But then the reason why actions—but not events—escape causal necessity when we view them noumenally cannot lie in their character qua performances of the agent, but in their noumenal, atemporal status. And Kant must still show why only actions— but not events—enjoy such a status. He must show, that is, why it is somehow more intelligible to talk about actions being performed in the noumenal sphere than it is to talk about events taking place in that sphere.

We will not pin down the required difference by insisting— as Kant often does—that some actions (but no events) issue *voluntarily* from the agent. For we still do not know why voluntary actions—and not brute events—are the most appropriate candidates for being the sources of new series of events. Everything we know about empirical actions and volitions suggests the opposite—for they too occur in time and must therefore be causally determined. Indeed, qua empirical, voluntary actions are themselves events: "voluntary actions, as events, have their determining ground in *antecedent* time";[16] and that means also in antecedent cause. This is why "the will of every man has an empirical character" (*CPR* A549, B577)—that is, a set of character traits, propensities, and dispositions to act supplying the causal background of all his voluntary actions. If, therefore, voluntary actions (but no events) are to be independent of causal determination, they must enjoy that independence not because they issue from man's will but because they issue from man's noumenal self. But then the initial difficulty reappears at once, for we are still not told why in that noumenal sphere— totally unknown to us anyway—only acts of will (but not events) are to be regarded as sources of new series of events.

In still other passages Kant seems to be suggesting that the origination of a sequence of events amounts to nothing short of a creatio ex nihilo on a minor scale; and any such creatio ex nihilo can be accomplished only by an act of free spontaneity of a self. Thus, when we want to talk about the origination of a chain of events we ought to talk about "An *original* act, such as can by itself bring about what did not exist before" (*CPR* A544, B572). The last part of the sentence clearly indicates that the origination of a series of events is tantamount to the creation of something radically *new* with respect to what existed thus far; such an act of creation, Kant adds in the same sentence, "is not to be looked for in the causally connected appearances" (ibid.). The reason for this last claim is clear: since the effect is fully determined by its cause(s), and since what is created by that "original act" represents an entirely new element with respect to everything that existed thus far, the "original act" is indeed creating ex nihilo and—if only for that reason—must escape the grip of causal necessity. How, we may ask further, are we to understand the occurrence of that "original act" itself? Kant's answer is, again, couched in a semitheological language: we must, he says, "admit the occurrence of self-caused events, that is, generation through *freedom*" (*CPR* A488, B516). Thus the self's "original act" creates ex nihilo a new sequence of events and is itself *causa sui*, that is, *free*.

What are we to make of this new turn in Kant's argument?

Taken as it stands, it is still insufficient to supply the grounds for attributing *freedom* to an item simply *originating* a new series of events. Granted, such an originating item must emerge independently of causal necessity; it still does not follow from this that such an item would have to be "caused by itself." Hume already pointed out the non-sequitur which destroys Kant's present move[17]—but then it is simply impossible to believe that Kant could have committed such a gross mistake.

Perhaps, then, it is unfair to Kant to take these passages merely as they stand, i.e., without considering their broader context. In all probability they are the echoes of an argument that Kant presented in his Observation on the Third Antinomy. In the Observation, the main argument of the thesis was interpreted by Kant himself (*CPR* A448–50, B476–78) as boiling down to the two following points: (1) In order to make intelligible the origin of the world as a whole (i.e., as the totality of its states, each of which is causally determined by the preceding state) we must admit the existence of the world's free and spontaneous cause; (2) since we are thereby forced to admit the existence of a free power of originating sequences of events making up the world as a whole, we may as well grant the possibility of there being such spontaneous beginnings *within* the world—and these would be the work of substances in the world (*CPR* A450, B478), that is, the work of free human agents (originating, within their modest means, new series of events).

Let us grant Kant as much as we can. Let us not object, for the moment, to (1) even though this "is largely a repetition of the Aristotelian-Thomistic proof of the impossibility of an infinite series of causes and hence of the necessity of a first cause."[18] Let us assume, then, that Kant has succeeded in conflating freedom and origination in the case of the divine being responsible for the creation of the world as a whole. Let us grant further that if it makes sense to ascribe such origination in freedom to the world as a whole, then it may also be legitimate to ascribe such an origination to a sequence of events beginning within the world. We still fall short of our target, for we have been offered no reason at all why new sequences of (worldly) events may not originate equally well in acts of freedom, and in some brute and unintelligible events. And the inevitably

noumenal status of the action of a first cause[19] gives us no reason
to prefer here free actions over (uncaused) events.

To sum up, the connection between the power to *originate* a
new series of events and the capacity to do so *freely* remains
unproved.

In the end, and in a truly last-ditch effort, Kant falls back
upon our notion of moral agency in hope of giving some
grounds to that connection between origination and freedom
he has been pressing on us all along. It is, he now tells us (*CPR*
A547, B575), "evident from the *imperatives*" of morality that
reason has the power of determining our conduct. Reason, that
is, has the power to make us act in conformity with what *ought*
to be rather than merely adapt ourselves to what is or will be due
to the operation of the causal laws governing the unfolding of
events; this is why we can be blamed or praised for our deeds.
Reason must thus be able to break the grip of causal necessity,
i.e., to act freely. It is, therefore, qua free, that reason will be able
to originate (in man's action insofar as it is rational) a sequence
of events. "Reason therefore acts *freely*. . . . This freedom . . .
must also be described in positive terms, as the power of
originating a series of events" (*CPR* A553, B581; A554, B582;
my emphasis).

But this way of conflating origination and freedom is due
entirely to Kant's reliance upon our notion of moral agency. "In
view of these considerations" (*CPR* A548, B576)—that is, in
view of what is implied by the notion of moral agency—Kant
does indeed succeed in welding together the concepts of origination and freedom. But Kant was also telling us, at an earlier
stage of his argument, that "the practical concept of freedom is
based on this *transcendental idea*" (*CPR* A533, B501)—that is
on the theoretical (albeit still "problematic," still devoid of any
objective reference) concept of freedom. And so for the idea of
moral agency to be admitted, we must first prove that the concept it is based on (the theoretical concept of a free origination
of a sequence of events) can be defended in its own right. Now
while it might be that Kant has reached his goal of proving that
such a concept "is at least *not incompatible with* nature" (*CPR*,
A558, B586), he has not proved why this concept's two key
components—origination and freedom—imply each other
quite independently of any of his "considerations" of the specifi-

cally moral features of human agency. Yet to prove this, was the task that Kant himself set up. It might be that for moral action to be possible the (noumenal) origin of a series of events must also be regarded as free; but the argument of the Third Antinomy intends to convince us that when we regard in this way the relationship between origination and freedom we are not deluded, but we find ourselves on sure and tested grounds at least insofar as our *concepts* are concerned: "The idea of freedom as a faculty of absolute spontaneity was not just a desideratum but, as far as its possibility was concerned, an *analytical principle* of *pure speculation*."[20] This is a big claim indeed! If it is to hold, Kant must show how the very ideas of origination and freedom are linked up by a conceptual necessity independently of any consideration of various claims of the pure practical reason (i.e., of morality). By completing itself with the certainties of pure practical reason, "speculative reason *does not herewith grow in insight* but only in respect to the certitude of its problematic concept of freedom."[21] We are entitled, therefore, to expect the articulation of that "insight" already within the framework of the problematic concept of freedom put forward by the *Critique of Pure Reason*. Unfortunately, no such insight is to be gained from a careful study of Kant's moves.

We have, at the beginning of this section, supplied the answer Kant's analysis has failed to produce. We have shown how the ideas of freedom and origination are indeed welded together as the conditions of inevitability and necessity in the world. For the notion of inevitability and necessity in the unfolding of events leads to the notion of sequences of events which we cannot hold at bay or absorb. But such sequences of events originate in the acts of human freedom—in the acts of the other as he deploys a purposeful, creative activity, where the past does not determine the shape of things to come, and where what is to come is determined through the sustained exercise of the other's creativity and inventiveness. In addition—and this is the answer to the first question that was raised in connection with the thesis's (and Kant's) way of defending freedom—this human capacity of originating new series of events is not at all posited on the grounds of a pseudo-argument concocted in order to escape the inacceptability of admitting an "infinite series" of events. The events' origination in freedom is an actual fact of an actual form of life: of our own form of life as it plays itself out in a violent world. Freedom as the "first cause" of a causal chain is not a mere "resting place for . . . imagination," unable to picture the "enigma" (CPR A449, B477) of an infinite series of effects and causes; on the contrary, the actuality of this freedom is the very *Realitätsprinzip* that draws the line for me between what I merely imagine or wish to be and what actually—that is, inexorably and inevitably—takes place.[22]

It is true that our acknowledgment of the existence and the effectiveness of freedom in the empirical world spells the end of the unchallenged rule of causal necessity in that world; and it is also true that Kant intended to avoid this outcome. But this intention, one must immediately point out, remains at odds with the actual state of affairs generated by his own theory.

In a nutshell, this is what happens when Kant gets down to the business of removing the incompatible standing of freedom and necessity in relation to each other. Kant's aim is to formulate what he intends to be a form of compatibilism; and his compatibilism is based on what is, in effect—and even in Kant's own words (CPR A543, B571)—a version of the double-aspect theory. Now while this theory may perhaps allow for a certain kind of reconciliation of the conflicting claims of freedom and necessity, the theory does not allow one to reconcile these conflicting claims as they have been formulated by Kant himself in the Third Antinomy. Whereas the theory does justice to the claims of the antithesis, it does not do justice to the claims of the thesis; for the defender of the thesis intends to convince us that the concept of freedom is applicable in and to the empirical world, while the Kantian solution removes freedom to the shadowy realm of "noumena." In point of fact, however—and this is the next circumstance we must note in connection with the general trend of Kant's solution—Kant himself is, in the end, unsuccessful in restricting the claims of the thesis to the world of noumena. He cannot escape the need to apply the concept of freedom to the ordinary, empirical realm and he thereby undercuts the framework of his compatibilism. In the last analysis he allows, or is forced to allow, for the intervention of freedom within the empirical world. As having an impact *upon* that world, freedom breaks out of its noumenal area of confinement and emerges suddenly *in* the empirical world, from which it was supposed to be banished once and for all.

Let us start by trying to get some grip on Kant's attempt to reconcile freedom and necessity. As we remember from our earlier analysis of Kant's position, a human action must be, qua empirical, subject to causal necessity. But—and this is the key idea of Kant's compatibilism—the very same action may also be viewed as caused by freedom. One and the same action, that is, is the effect of two entirely different causes belonging to two entirely different orders of reality and conception. There can be no conflict between these two different causes for there is no area, Kant contends, where they could enter into competition and clash with each other. Each can exercise its authority without in the least infringing upon the territory of the other.

The key premise in that solution is, of course, Kant's distinction between the phenomenal (the sensible) and the noumenal (the intelligible) realms. He has argued for that distinction earlier in the *Critique*[23] and he is therefore justified in appealing to it at this stage of his argument. The noumenal realm—which we cannot know but can at least "think" due to our use of unschematized categories—is not subject to, among other things, the form of time. Insofar, then, as human actions can be thought of as originating outside of time, they can also be thought of as escaping the grip of causal necessity; for, as we remember, while we have sufficient reasons to believe that all temporal phenomena are governed by causal necessity, we have, by the same token and due to the same consideration, no reason at all to believe that the rule of causal necessity extends over nontemporal areas. And this leaves an opening for our actions' total independence of causal necessity. To be sure, we cannot *know* them to be so independent, but then it is not Kant's aim to produce such knowledge. All he needs to show is the possibility of freedom; its actuality (and even then only as a requirement of morality) will not dawn upon us until and unless we take into account our notion of moral agency.

An important piece of evidence is still missing from Kant's case as we have presented it so far. "The effects of . . . an intelligible cause appear, and accordingly can be determined through other appearances, but its causality is not so determined. While the effects are to be found in the series of empirical conditions, the intelligible cause, together with its causality, is outside the series. Thus the effect may be regarded as free in respect of its intelligible cause, and at the same time in respect of appearances as resulting from them according to the necessity of nature" (*CPR* A537, B565). But why should we view *man*—indeed man alone—as such an intelligible, and hence free, cause of his actions? Kant does have an answer to this question. A cause is intelligible if it "has in itself a faculty which is not an object of sensible intuition" (*CPR* A538, B566). Now man does have such a nonsensible faculty, for though he "knows all the rest of nature solely through senses, [he] knows himself also through pure apperception" (*CPR* A546, B574). Man thus has a supersensible, intelligible self and, for this reason, human actions can be viewed as originating outside of time and hence also outside of the iron grip of causal necessity. On the other hand, however, the very same actions, when viewed as items in the phenomenal, empirical world must be seen as being fully and completely determined by their natural causes.

We can see immediately why this double-aspect theory amounts to a sacrifice of the thesis. For the thesis did not argue for the proposition that events, apart from being subject to the "causality of nature" are *also* subject to the "causality of freedom." The thesis argued for a more radical view: that at least some events in the world are caused *only* by the acts of freedom and *not at all* (and not in any "respect") by the causality of nature. Kant's solution, therefore, is slanted heavily toward the antithesis: insofar as our knowledge of the world is concerned, the deterministic position turns out to be the winning one.

But this triumph of the antithesis spells the defeat of Kant's *own* aim to save freedom; and since Kant is not prepared to give up on the aim, his own solution is, ultimately, unstable. Freedom, chased out of the empirical world, returns to it through the back door.

In the first place—and to take the difficulty at its most general level—it is quite impossible to talk about freedom as that power of originating "a series occurring *in the world*" (*CPR* A450, B478) and, at the same time, persist in confining freedom to the noumenal sphere. For according to Kant's own terminology, events take place in the phenomenal, empirical world; and so if freedom is the causal power behind some events, these events must bear certain identifiable—visible and tangible, as it were—traces of their origin. Of Kant's "noumenal" freedom it must be said what Hegel will say later about Essence (*Wesen*) in general:

Essence must appear (*Das Wesen muss erscheinen*). But if this is to
be the case, then Kant's entire compatibilist project must, and
will, break down. For then the occurrence of events will not be
due to two independent and peacefully coexisting kinds of
causes; some of these events will turn out to be caused by nature
but *not* by freedom while some of them will turn out to be
caused by freedom but *not* by nature. If freedom is to have an
impact in the phenomenal world, free actions—and the chains
of events originating in those actions—must represent a positive break in the rule of causal necessity in *that* world.

This general observation can easily be made more specific.
The "transcendental idea of freedom" was indispensable, Kant
was telling us, to our making sense of the notion of *imputability*
of actions (*CPR* A448, B476). That is, prior to and as the
condition of our moral discourse we must find ourselves in
possession of some grounds on which we impute an action to an
agent; and these grounds, Kant holds, involve our sense of the
action's issuing freely from the agent. Now when we use this
(plainly and empirically understood) expression we take for
granted our (plainly and empirically exercised) ability to mark
off actions freely performed by the agent from all kinds of things
that happen to and with the agent but that are not done freely by
him. All of this is a matter of logical necessity: if imputation
implies freedom of the agent, then no imputation is warranted
unless this—but not that or that—particular occurrence is
empirically recognized as a free action. And so when Kant talks
about imputability we witness the spectacle of the philosopher
sliding back into the very position he has been trying to abandon: "If, for instance, I at this moment arise from my chair, in
complete freedom, without being necessarily determined there-
to by the influence of natural causes . . . a new series . . . has its
absolute beginning in this event. . . . For this resolution and act
of mine do not form parts of succession of purely natural effects. . . . natural causes exercise over it no determining influence whatsoever. It does indeed follow upon them, but without
arising out of them" (*CPR* A451, B479). Several plain and
empirical things are assumed by this passage to be plainly and
empirically identifiable. I know that my present action of getting up from my chair is performed freely and without any
"influence of natural causes"; clearly, then, in all kinds of differ-

ent situations I could be getting up from my chair *under* the influence of those "natural causes" and therefore not freely at all. If, say, someone were to run a burst of electric current through that chair, then the sudden upward movement of my body would definitely not be a free action. While my free action of getting up from the chair does indeed begin a new series of events (ibid.), my jumping up from the electrically charged seat is simply a link in a chain of events already taking place. When I get up freely from that chair "this resolution and act of mine. . . . does indeed follow upon [natural causes], but without arising out of them"—for example, I may feel the need to stretch my legs, but it is not the need itself which *makes me* get up from that chair—while in that second example the sudden shock of an unbearable pain makes my body jerk up in the air. Freedom and causal necessity are now the two competing accounts of what takes place in the empirical world and as empirically identifiable phenomena.

It is not possible to object that since the passage we have just considered is to be found in the Observation on the thesis it should not be used as an illustration of the difficulty inherent in Kant's later attempt to reconcile the thesis and the antithesis. For the position of the thesis on the imputability of actions is indistinguishable from Kant's own; and so the difficulty re-emerges within Kant's own view. In effect, if imputability is logically dependent upon freedom and if we impute empirical (and empirically identifiable) pieces of human behavior, then freedom too must exhibit empirical (and empirically identifiable) marks. And so, once again—and quite predictably—we see Kant adopting a mode of expression incompatible with his compatibilism, as when he talks about the causality of our will "which, independently of . . . natural causes, and even contrary to their force and influence" (*CPR* A543, B567), can intervene in the world and produce a new series of events. This position—the position Kant is driven to adopt—is indistinguishable, even in its wording, from the thesis and, as we just saw, it cannot be squared with Kant's decision to lock up freedom in the noumenal realm.

We can arrive at exactly the same conclusion by examining Kant's crucial distinction between the agent's *intelligible* and *empirical* character. The possession of an empirical character is not a specifically human privilege: every efficient cause must have such a character (*CPR* A539, B567) insofar as every efficient cause produces only certain kinds of effects. What kind of effects they are depends on the dispositional structure of the cause; due to its heaviness my iron axe will produce such and such effects which will be completely different from the effects produced by the brittle glass on my shelf, etc. Similarly, every human agent will also perform the kinds of actions which are determined by the causal background of his empirical character. Thus, if we know the agent's empirical character we will be able to explain why this or that natural inclination causes, inevitably, this or that action. In the case of human agents, though, this empirical character qualifies them only qua members of the empirical, phenomenal world. As noumenal, intelligible beings, human agents are endowed with an *intelligible* character and this character is also the intelligible (that is, free) cause of their actions.

How are we to understand this relationship of the empirical and the intelligible character in a human agent? It is at this point that the contradiction in Kant's theory of freedom reemerges. On the one hand, the intelligible character is said to be totally unknown to us, for it is nothing other than man's noumenal self, i.e., his "character as thing in itself" (ibid.). On the other hand, however, the intelligible character serves as the intelligible and free cause of human actions—and these are the same actions that take place in the phenomenal world governed by causal necessity. The intelligible character, then, is having a clear impact upon the empirical world; thus there are (and we must be able to identify) certain phenomena which manifest that intelligible character and which, therefore, must bear some marks and traces of its presence. And so we find Kant drifting away from his initial sharp separation of the intelligible character and the empirical character: the latter is now to serve as the "sensible sign" (*CPR* A546, B574) of the former, or else as its "sensible scheme" (*CPR* A553, B581), etc. The very expressions that Kant is here forced to adopt indicate the nature of the difficulty. If the intelligible character's dwelling place is in the noumenal, supersensible realm, then nothing phenomenal and sensible *can* be a sign of it. Whereas a pure category of understanding can indeed be schematized—by receiving a temporal interpretation—the intelligible character cannot. If we could schematize it, we would have to count it as belonging to our *knowledge*—both as a concept and as an object corresponding to that concept—and this would be incompatible with the intelligible character's noumenal status and hence also with its freedom, since nothing except noumena can escape the grip of causal necessity. The contradiction in Kant's position is clear: in one and the same breath we are told about the intelligible character that "we do not know [it]; we can only indicate its nature by means of appearances" (*CPR* A551, B579). But if we *can* indicate the intelligible character's nature by means of appearances, then—however mysterious that "indication" must remain, given Kant's premises—we most certainly *do* know something about the intelligible character. If, further, we can impute an action to the agent only if we know that action to be freely performed, and if an action is considered freely performed only when viewed as issuing from man's intelligible character, then the reason why I discriminate between—to return to the earlier examples—my getting up freely from the chair and my body's jumping up from it when hit with electric current is based, ultimately, on my ability to grasp empirically the manifestations of my intelligible character. This is another route along which freedom—both in my own case and in the case of all agents to whom I am prepared to impute actions—makes its way back to the empirical world. Freedom thus enters again in direct competition with causal necessity and—as Kant is driven to acknowledge—it clearly wins that competition at least in some cases.

Kant's programmatic confinement of freedom to the noumenal sphere has highly undesirable consequences for our ability to identify empirically not only the agents' free actions, but those very free agents themselves. Here Fichte's old objection remains perfectly valid and pertinent.[24] Kant's argument in the Third Antinomy gives us no grounds for attaching the noumenal freedom only to those phenomenal objects (the human bodies) that are endowed with such and such—and not any other—features and characteristics. When talking about the "intelligible cause" of phenomena, Kant begins and conducts his argument in the terminology which—given the overall framework of the first *Critique*—is applicable to anything and everything in experience, and not to human beings alone. Kant first points out that "if appearances are things in themselves" (*CPR* A536, B564)—if, that is, the phenomenal world is the ultimate and the only reality there is—then freedom cannot be defended, for the realm of appearances has already been proved to be in the grip of causal necessity. Fortunately for us, Kant goes on, appearances are not things in themselves but only our representations and they thus—qua representations—demand some grounds which are not themselves representations (*CPR* A537, B565). To put it differently, appearances must be viewed as originating in something that is not itself an appearance. Precisely this ground of appearances is called by Kant their "intelligible cause" (ibid.) and the mode of causation exercised by that cause—that is, the "causality of a thing in itself" (*CPR* A538, B566)—is nothing other than the causality of freedom.

But—and this is the gist of Fichte's objection—if the distinction between phenomena and things in themselves (noumena) is quite general and if the latter are totally unknown to us anyway, then on what grounds do we attribute the noumenal power of acting freely only to the phenomenon of a *human* shape? According to Kant, man and man alone is to be regarded as the intelligible cause of appearances because man is the only creature "which in the sensible world must be regarded as appearance [and yet] has in itself a faculty which is not an object of sensible intuition" (ibid.). But if we do not know the noumenal, intelligible side of appearances anyway—if indeed the very difference between the mental and the material may not be operative in things in themselves (*CPR* A358–360)—then how do we know if the body of a pet of ours (to take Fichte's example) is not to be viewed as also endowed with noumenal freedom? If in knowing "himself through pure apperception" (*CPR* A546, B574) man is to himself "a purely intelligible object" (*CPR* A547, B575)—that is, as Kant told us a moment ago, a thing in itself—then there is no reason why, in the noumenal order of things, pure apperception could not be attributed to Fichte's pet just as validly as we attribute it to other humans.

To conclude: as an empirically identifiable activity, freedom must be attributed to empirical and empirically identifiable agents. And this is exactly how freedom appeared to us at the beginning of the present section. Freedom did not emerge as a mysterious noumenal capacity to be superadded, somehow, upon the phenomenal shape of human individuals. Freedom was simply a way of acting of those individuals—of the human power-centers mobilizing their brains and their muscles, their skills and their tools—as they drive their vital powers to ever higher levels of creativity. We have also seen how man as such a free, creative agent becomes an inescapable danger to other men.

It befell to Hegel to make the first systematic attempt at articulating the connection between freedom and violence. But Kant himself came amazingly close to recognizing its pivotal importance, and not simply in (and for) his moral philosophy—where the ever possible choice of Evil is the indispensable condition of a *free* commitment to the moral law[25]—but in the very treatment of the "transcendental freedom" in the Third Antinomy of Pure Reason. In setting up the argument of the antithesis Kant shows clear awareness of the awesome price to be paid for the admission of freedom. For freedom is not simply liberation from causal necessity, it is also "a liberation . . . from the guidance of all rules." We cannot say, Kant continues, that there are some "*laws* of freedom" taking the place of "natural laws." For if there were such laws of freedom then freedom would simply be "nature under another name." And so, Kant concludes, "Nature and transcendental freedom differ as do conformity to law and *lawlessness*" (*CPR* A447, B475; my emphasis).

Now, it is obviously true—Kant's entire moral philosophy is a monument to this truth—that there can be, and there are in fact, certain laws within which freedom can express itself. But if the freedom that commits itself to follow its (self-imposed) law—the law of the categorical imperative—is to remain free (if, in Kant's words, it is not to be "nature by another name"), then it can never lose its capacity to *repudiate its own law* by becoming "lawless." Only then *reasons* to act are not causes of action under a different name. Now the law of freedom—the categorical imperative—means respect of fellow human beings and of oneself as a member of the human community. The repudiation of this law, therefore, is tantamount to the repudiation by man of his bond of fellowship with other men and of his own status as a member of the human community. In the last analysis—and in Hegel's analysis as well—such a repudiation can be nothing other than an option for violence.

IV.   The Enduring Self

Several strands of the argument that we have been pursuing coalesce around the notion of the self. In violence, the other emerges as the ultimate limit of my powers; his position towards me is the one of an "indivisible" and truly "particular" power center. Now insofar as he *endures* in his capacity of my ultimate limit, and insofar as the sheer "thisness" of the power center that he is *continues* to elude the grip of my powers, the other imposes himself upon me as an enduring and continuing self. And this status of his as a true continuant is just as primitive and underived as his status of a true bearer of properties. I need no criteria to justify my belief in the enduring identity of my adversary in the life-and-death struggle, for I cannot conceive this struggle otherwise than as played out among the participants capable of enduring as this or that particular power center. On the contrary, here as in our other cases my search for criteria takes place only when I abstract from the background of violent relations among men; and, inevitably, such a search can yield no results. There can be no criteria for something being a constant and enduring self, since such constancy and endurance are primitive terms imposed upon me in an original experience: the experience of a human agent continuing and enduring in his capacity of my ultimate limit.

Neither is it the case that the corresponding conception of *myself* emerges through a different channel. To the extent that I am defined by a violent world, I am thrown back upon myself: nothing in that world gives me a secure protection against the other, and so I find myself "all by myself," disentangled from all the ties and attachments ordinarily defining my identity for me. Thus to endure the trial of violence is to endure it "all by myself"—and this is how I first gain the conception of myself as an enduring self set apart from everything outside me. Already at the dawn of modern philosophy, in the thinking of Descartes, some glimpses into the background of violence as that soil from which our idea of the self is derived can clearly be detected. For if—as I have already argued elsewhere[26]—Descartes' "evil demon" represents the personification of *human* threats deployed against an individual and if—as Descartes himself argues—a human individual is thrown back upon himself due to the menace of the evil demon, then in Descartes too the self first gains its separate identity by collecting itself from, and enduring against, a violent environment.

This implies, immediately, that my own identity as an enduring self—in that Cartesian modern sense of the term—cannot be established outside of a relation of violence to other such selves. Insofar as I collect myself from the world, I do it under the threat of the other; and so my reality and my conception of myself as an enduring self imply the reality and the conception of my adversaries.

The reemergence of this idea in the philosophy of Hegel is what I shall outline in the present section. I shall not be, therefore, attempting to break any new ground in this section; rather, I shall try to let the theme of "enduring self" develop of its own momentum beginning with its complete suppression at the hands of Hume.

Let us briefly review Hume's basic terms. Our "perceptions"—all our mental contents, that is—can be divided into "impressions" and "ideas." Among the impressions we must count "sensations, passions and emotions,"[27] while ideas are the sorts of items (thoughts, images, etc.) we employ in "thinking and reasoning."[28] Impressions are easily distinguishable from ideas due to their "force and vivacity." All simple ideas—all simple thoughts, conceptions, images, etc.—are derived from their corresponding impressions; complex ideas alone need not have such a direct origin in impressions, for any complex idea might well have been produced by the free play of our thought and imagination.

Given that all of our perceptions are either impressions or ideas, our identical "self" might first be viewed[29] as something that is immediately *felt* by us, that is as an impression. In this case, we would need no proof of the existence of our self, since all impressions carry with them all the force and vivacity required to induce belief in their reality. Such an immediate and immediately given feeling of the self would be, one could further suggest, present in all of our perceptions, whatever they might be. On the one hand, our passions, emotions, and sensations would always carry with them (because of the influence they exercise upon us through pain and pleasure) some connection with the feeling of our self. On the other hand, there could be no conception, no thought, and hence no demonstrative proof of anything if we doubted the reality of the self. Thus the existence of the self would be given in any and every mental content we are capable of experiencing.

But, Hume objects, there is no feeling of the self to be found in a careful introspection of our mental life, "nor have we any idea of *self* after the manner it is here explain'd";[30] indeed this second denial follows from Hume's rejection of the first claim. For as we have no feeling of the self—in other terms, we have no *impression* of the self as an enduring and invariable item preserving its identity throughout our changing perceptions—the alleged idea of the self finds no corresponding impression from which it could have been derived. To put it differently, the idea of a constant and invariable self would have to be derived from a constant and invariable impression; and as no such impression can be found anywhere in our mental experience, it is not surprising that our introspection fails to hit upon such an impression of the self. There is *no* invariable and constant (uninterrupted) impression present in the course of our lives; and that is sufficient to prove that the corresponding conception of our self lacks the supporting evidence.

In point of fact, however, Hume's claim is even more radical than that. It is not simply that we have no invariable and uninterrupted impression of the self, but we do not find *any* impression of the self at *any* moment of our mental lives. As Hume puts it in his famous metaphor: "The mind is a kind of theatre, where several perceptions successively make their appearance; pass, re-pass, glide away and mingle in an infinite variety of postures and situations. . . . The comparison of the theatre must not mislead us. They are the successive perceptions only, that constitute the mind; nor have we the most distant notion of the place, where these scenes are represented, or of the materials, of which it is compose'd."[31] These perceptions, let us add, are all distinguishable and different from each other; they may thus be considered separately—and since everything that may be con-

sidered separately is capable of a separate existence, there is no
necessary unity among the perceptions making up a particular
mind. Every mind, therefore, is only a "bundle or collection of
different perceptions."[32] We are at the very antipodes of the
Leibnizian metaphysics where each and every mental experience
of a self expresses that self's complete individual notion and
where, therefore, all perceptions' link with each other and with
the self they all belong to is secured by a necessary law. Even a
contingent relation of perceptions to a "self" is out of the question for Hume, since there simply *is* no self over and above a
bundle of perceptions lumped together in a certain way. And so
when the "metaphysicians" that Hume fulminates against persist in talking not only about the self but about its perfect
"identity" and "simplicity" they do so by departing from the
available data: "There is properly no *simplicity* in [mind] at one
time, nor *identity* in different."[33] Let us consider these two
notions—of simplicity and identity—one by one.

When Hume talks here about "simplicity," he has in mind
two things. First, the mental data at our disposal are such that at
no moment is the "theatre" we call our mind filled by a simple
perception: at any of these moments we have some impressions
of the senses going together with, say, some emotions, or passions, or recollections, and so on. Second, and more important,
the various elements of a perception are not linked together by
any necessary law; they are all distinguishable and separable
from each other in our imagination, and they are thus capable of
a separate existence. While a Leibnizian could easily accommodate the first claim—in fact, he would never even dream of
challenging it—he would vigorously repudiate the second
claim: since, for Leibniz, every perception *as a whole* is a necessary episode in the life of the self (the "monad") that owns it, all
elements of every perception are linked by a necessary law. And
so Hume is definitely not fighting a straw man when he dis-
agrees with the "metaphysicians of this kind."[34]

The idea of our selves' identity through time does not fare
any better. There is no impression from which this idea could
have been derived and so the idea is fictitious through and
through. When we carefully inspect our mental scene we see
that everything there is in a state of "perpetual flux and movement."[35] We do not have—as would be required if our con-

ception of the self as identical through time were to be a sound
one—the impression of an invariable and uninterrupted self.
Quite apart from the fact that I never have an impression of a
"self," whatever impressions I do have exhibit only change and
interruptedness.

Since the idea of a self endowed with identity through different times and simplicity at one time cannot be traced back to our
impressions, this idea must be deemed illegitimate. It is not to
be found *in* our experiences but is attributed by us *to* them. The
only question still left to ask is how we came to form such an
idea. And this is indeed the question that Hume now asks.

The answer is arrived at along the same route Hume has
already tested in his earlier analyses of continued and distinct
existence and of substance in general. "[A] single object, plac'd
before us, and survey'd for any time without our discovering
any interruption or variation, is able to give us a notion of
identity."[36] We have seen that nothing like this was to be found
in the "theatre" of our mind, where perceptions are in a state of
variation and interruptedness. Thus the data that are here displayed to our contemplation warrant only our idea of diversity.
However, when taken jointly with a certain natural disposition
or propensity of our imagination, these data will induce us to
form the idea of an identical self. In effect, these variable and
interrupted perceptions that we do see in the theater of our
mind are so closely related to each other, and our imagination
slides so smoothly along them, that it easily mistakes them for
the perceptions of an identical self.[37] Hume's account of the
self's simplicity proceeds along the same route.[38]

What remains to be done is to show just how the three
principles of association of ideas—contiguity, resemblance, and
the relation of cause and effect—induce our imagination to slide
easily along certain stretches of mental data and to organize
them into a "self." Hume finds no role for contiguity in this area
and so the entire notion of personal identity is said to emerge
from a cooperation of resemblance and causality.

The resemblance here at issue is, above all, the resemblance
between a recollection and what that recollection is of. Memory
offers us innumerable images of our past perceptions and, as
nothing is more similar than an image and the object that image
is meant to represent for us, our imagination, when sliding

along sequences of our recollections of past perceptions, quite
naturally mistakes their diversity for their unity in an identical
self. It is not that both the past perceptions and their present
recollections are discovered as *already* belonging to one and the
same self (although, obviously, memory performs this more
modest task too); rather, by being presented with a set of present and past perceptions so closely resembling each other, our
memory and our imagination actually produce the idea of an
identical self. This association by resemblance is strengthened
by the association through causality. In the first place, and quite
obviously, my present perceptions are all viewed as belonging to
my self even though they resemble neither each other nor (since
in most cases they are not recollections of my past) my past
perceptions. In the second place, I have perceptions of certain
future events as anticipated episodes in my life history; this is
why the thought of them may give me the feeling of pain or
pleasure. In all these cases, all of these perceptions belong to the
bundle that I call "myself" due to their *causal* connection with
each other and with other members of that particular bundle.
Indeed Hume seems to be putting forward an idea of the mind
as a system of perceptions where all perceptions stand in causal
connections: "the *true idea* of the human mind is to consider it
as a system of different perceptions or different existences,
which are link'd together by the relation of cause and effect, and
mutually produce, destroy, influence and modify each other."[39]
However, were this to be the "true idea" of the mind, then
association through resemblance would have to play, at the very
best, an auxiliary role. The resemblance between our recollections and our past perceptions would perhaps remain the
starting point of a mental process from which the idea of the self
would to emerge; but even in the cases of very clear resemblance
between perceptions the truly important work would have to be
done by causality: my past perception P would not contribute to
the formation of the idea of my self due to P's resemblance with
recollections of it, but due to P's causal connections with other
perceptions. The key role thus attributed to causal relations
would be fully in line with Hume's own earlier assessment of the
strength of these relations as compared with contiguity and
resemblance. When I think of my past, I think of something that
really took place, of something that induces me to *believe* in its

existence some time ago. But Hume has already argued[40] that both contiguity and resemblance have such a weak and uncertain influence upon the mind, that they are, for all intents and purposes, incapable of inducing us to believe in anything lying beyond the narrow boundaries of our present impressions. Only causality has the required "force and constancy"[41] to induce any such belief—and hence also the belief in the reality of our personal past.

Furthermore, causality has a special job to do which memory could not do in any case. In effect, there are many episodes in my mental history which I do not remember—and yet I attribute them unhesitatingly to myself. We may presume too—although Hume does not actually say it—that such nonremembered stretches of experience must also go into the very process of producing the idea of the self, since, quite evidently, our idea of a human self is not the idea of an all-remembering self.

Now, our memory gaps do not undercut our belief in the identity of our self insofar as they are filled with the aid of causation. For example, I may not remember how I got from A to D on the freeway—I might have been daydreaming—but having now the perception of D and knowing full well that I could not have gotten from A to D without having driven through B and C, I know that that forgotten stretch of the trip is part and parcel of my personal history.

In assessing Hume's account one must ask two fundamental questions: (1) Can we account for our idea of the self, given the kinds of data that Hume told us are to be the building materials for that idea? (2) Can Hume explain—without assuming the very same idea of the self he is supposed to account for—why it is that those data present themselves to us the way they do?

Everything I will now say in response to these two questions is borrowed directly from Barry Stroud's *Hume*.[42]

1. In response to the first question, then, it is easy to come up with counterexamples to Hume's attempt at deriving the idea of the self from the resemblance between various perceptions. According to Hume, our memory does not merely discover perceptions as belonging to one and the same self, but produces the idea of such a self to begin with. Certain perceptions are lumped together into "my self" not because they are retained in what is already my memory—the concept of *my* memory is what

we have to explain in the first place—but because of a mere resemblance between recollection and its object. Now suppose—to take Stroud's example—that we imagine a series of perceptions which are all, without exception, perceptions of the Eiffel Tower viewed from one particular distance, angle, and the like. Qualitatively, these perceptions are indistinguishable, and so our imagination slides easily along them; but we do not, nevertheless, think of them as belonging to one person. And yet it is clear that the resemblance between all of these perceptions is much greater than the resemblance between any one of them and all other mental experiences of the person (this or that tourist or passerby, etc.) to whom we attribute that particular perception. It is not possible to reply to this by saying that the condition under which we can ascribe resemblance to a series of perceptions is that they occur all in one particular person's memory; for then it is memory, not resemblance, that must do the job—and yet we have no right, so far, to employ the concept of a "particular person's memory."

Do we fare any better by supplementing our account with the relation of causality? To answer this question in the affirmative one would have to show at least two things: (*a*) that there could be no causal chain of perceptions belonging to different persons and (*b*) that all perceptions belonging to one person are connected by the causal relation. The first claim is dubious, the second is outright false.[43]

2. In response to the second question, one must first note that Hume's task is to account for our idea of the self in a nonsolipsistic world, that is, in a world filled with different persons. Hume is fully aware of this, for even in the main section on personal identity he talks both about himself[44] *and* about others—as when he begins his argument on resemblance by saying "suppose we cou'd see clearly into the breast of another."[45] Since we cannot have the perceptions of others (or, to be more precise, we cannot inspect the bundles of perceptions which will go into the making of other minds), our idea of the self must be shown to arise from our mind's inspection of only some, but not all, perceptions occurring in the world. But just why it is that we can inspect only some, but not all, perceptions occurring in the world; and why it is that the perceptions we can inspect are not selected at random from the total set of perceptions occurring in

the world, but represent a determinate series such "that no member of a particular series could be a perception of any perception outside that series"?[46] If, as Hume claims, perceptions are distinguishable and separable in imagination and hence capable of a separate existence, then "why do perceptions present themselves, so to speak, in discrete, separate bundles? There seems to be no way for Hume to explain that basic fact about perceptions, although his genetic explanation of the origin of the idea of the self relies on it."[47]

The two difficulties that Hume's no-ownership theory[48] fails to resolve are quickly left behind us if we turn for philosophical guidance to Kant's *Critique of Pure Reason*. Both difficulties are eliminated by the repudiation of the entire framework that was bound to lead to them in the first place. Contrary to Hume, any representation which is to appear to me on the stage of that mental "theatre" that Hume talked about must already be thought of as *my* representation. Thus the idea of the self is prior to and necessary for our ability to entertain any representation whatsoever. In addition, the "I" that is so implied by each and every representation making up my mental scenery is, qua particular and finite, familiar only with a certain subset of the total set of representations occurring in the world. For Kant at least—although we need not go into details—these two claims are not logically independent. It is precisely because my mind is finite—and that means also *discursive*—that I find myself under a necessity to refer to my "thinking I" all the representations I am aware of.

Now for all this to be possible, both my I and the representations that are to be entertained by it must meet a number of criteria and exhibit a number of features. For example, as the owner of each and all of my representations, my I must have an identity through different times and a simplicity at one time. And if such features cannot indeed be detected in an introspective grasp of our mental experiences they must nevertheless be posited as a matter of conceptual necessity. But this conclusion does not mean a throwback to the pre-Humean positions of metaphysicians. For the conceptual necessity at issue does not allow us to make any substantive claims about the self. Since we lack—and inevitably so, as Kant will argue in the *Critique,* in the chapter on the Paralogisms—any intuition of our self, and since

no substantive cognitive claim about anything can be advanced
without our ability to back it up with an appropriate intuition,
our conception of the self as identical, simple, and so on, is a
mere logical function. "It must be possible for the 'I think' to
accompany all my representations" (*CPR* B131); but the thinking I that is thereby implied in each and every representation is
not the mental substance in the style of the old rationalistic
metaphysics of the soul. On the contrary, all metaphysical claims
about the self represent a "paralogism" of pure reason.

The traditional metaphysician—the "rational psychologist"
as he is called in the Paralogisms—has one thing in common
with Kant. He too attributes all representations to the "thinking
I," the *ego cogito*. He then zeroes in on the thinking I itself. The
"I think" is the "sole text" (*CPR* A343, B401) of the rational
psychologists as they "hypostatise" (*CPR* A384) that merely
formal conception of the self into a real entity and then go on to
attribute a number of features to it.

In his characterization of the "I think" Kant uses a bewilder-
ing array of terms. The "I think" is a "concept" or a "vehicle of
all concepts"; but then also a "representation" and "a bare consciousness which accompanies all concepts." As is usually the
case in the *Critique,* Kant's point is more likely to be obscured
than clarified if we attempt to sort out these competing concepts
(and their definitions) rather than focus on their actual uses in
Kant's argument. The chapter on the Paralogisms is no exception to that general rule. There is, however, one highly revealing
expression that Kant employs in this chapter's very opening
section; after having first subjected the reader to a merciless
terminological bombardment, Kant indicates that the conception of the self all four paralogisms proceed from is nothing
other than "the mere apperception '*I think*'" (*CPR* A343,
B401). And this, of course, is a term that every student of the
Transcendental Deduction must have become reasonably clear
about by now. When we pay heed to Kant's constant admoni-
tions in the Paralogisms to conceive that "I think" as a merely
formal and logical function attached to all representations, we
find ourselves brought back to the land Kant has already begun
to plough in the Transcendental Deduction.

For in the Transcendental Deduction—and especially in its
second edition—Kant has talked at some length about the "*an-*

alytic unity of apperception" (*CPR* B133). Such talk about an "analytic" unity of the self was warranted, Kant argued, since the underlying "principle of the necessary unity of apperception is itself, indeed, an identical, and therefore analytic, proposition" (*CPR* B135). These statements summarize what is in fact the main premise of the Transcendental Deduction—and hence also of the entire philosophical edifice Kant has erected. Every representation that I entertain, Kant contends, must be thought of as "mine." I can entertain mentally no concept (empirical or pure) and no intuition (empirical or pure) without viewing it as *my* concept or intuition. While it is true that the analytic unity of apperception presupposes its synthetic unity (*CPR* B133)—in other words, there would be no organized and integrated self if it were not for the transcendental activities of synthesis imposing necessary order upon the unstructured manifold of sensibility—it nevertheless remains the case that given our normal self, organized and integrated, it is unintelligible to talk about a representation which does not belong to the representing self. And so the self, albeit not given in a Humean "impression," must necessarily be posited as the owner of representations.

But—and this is the reason why the repudiation of Hume's no-ownership theory does not amount to the acceptance of the rationalistic doctrines of the self as a mental substance—the self we are led to posit as the owner of representations remains merely *formal*. All representations have the general (and necessary) form of belonging to the self; but, precisely for that reason, the self itself cannot be made into an object of any representation, and hence no substantive cognitive claims can be advanced about the nature of the self. All our attempts to advance any such claims about the self "can only revolve in a *perpetual circle*, since any judgment upon it has always already made use of its representation" (*CPR* A346, B404; my emphasis). There can be no doubt about Kant's stand here: it is precisely because our conception of the self "revolves *perpetually* in a *circle* [that] it does not help us in respect to any question which aims at synthetic knowledge" (*CPR* A366; my emphasis). I have emphasized this circular or self-referential feature of the "thinking I," as the latter attempts to represent itself, for this feature is unique to the self. Let us pay closer attention to this point. The "thinking I" can entertain and inspect mentally not only various empirical items—empirical concepts, intuitions, laws, and so on—but even pure concepts and pure intuitions. The case of pure intuitions is here easier to grasp and less controversial, at least given Kant's teaching about space and time in the Transcendental Aesthetic. Not only is our sensibility endowed with the necessary spatiotemporal frame for ordering sensory data; but, in addition, the general features of that frame itself are open to our inspection and description. It is true that for that inspection and description to be possible space and time must—and can—be exhibited in intuition; and it is also true that the pure concepts cannot be so intuited. Even so, however, they too can become explicitly represented in thought by the "thinking I" and the "I" can then grasp at least those of their determinations which will allow us to compose an ordered list of the pure categories, to establish various relations between the four main groups of the categories and between the three categories belonging to each group, etc. Indeed Kant goes so far as to say that the act of "I think" is "always included in the conceiving" (*CPR* A341, B399) of all transcendental (i.e., pure) concepts; what he means is that we could not employ the concepts of, say, substance or cause, without having some conception (with a minimum of determinateness) of these concepts' marks and features. To handle the concept of substance or of cause, we may say, one must have some notion of what these concepts are "all about." One must thus have an intellectual grasp of their determinations; and it is such a grasp of and by the "thinking I" that makes them altogether possible as our concepts (*CPR* A343, B401.

The "thinking I," in contrast, cannot attribute any determinations to *itself*—and this is due precisely to its circular, self-referential standing vis-à-vis itself. Any attempt to grasp the "I" as a determinate representation is still the work of the very same "I." The "I" is everywhere and, therefore, nowhere; whatever determinate representation of the "I" one may produce, that representation will not capture that "I" qua representing—it will be the representation of the *determinable* self, but not of the *determining* self (*CPR* B407). And it will be a strange representation indeed, since "there is nothing determinate in it" and we entertain it "without noting in it any quality whatsoever" (*CPR* A355).

Now, because rational psychology aims at producing substantive knowledge of the self while proceeding from "no other basis for this teaching than the simple, and in itself *completely empty,* representation 'I' " (*CPR* A346, B404; my emphasis) the entire project of the rational psychologist is doomed to failure. Having only an empty representation to work with, he will, inevitably, produce empty—that is merely tautological, trivial—statements for our consumption. He will then try to give these statements a substantive status and he will use them as premises justifying various substantive claims about the nature of the self. Such is the general structure of all four paralogisms: in each of them a perfectly valid but tautological statement about the form of "I" (the major premise) is suddenly given an unwarranted substantive interpretation (in the minor premise) and so the conclusion yields some substantive but equally unwarranted piece of information about the "soul"—that it is immaterial, immortal, and so on. All four paralogisms are, of course, transcendental and not formal: the invalid conclusion is due to a faulty transcendental ground smuggled into the minor premise. While in the major premise the "I" is still considered only as the mere form of representations, in the minor premise this very same "I" is suddenly taken as a real and knowable entity (the "soul"), that is, as the sort of entity to which both the pure and the empirical concepts can be validly applied. The rational psychologist is then in a position to offer us—in the conclusion—his pseudo-insights into the nature of the soul.

In what follows I will not be concerned with Kant's sustained struggle with the rational psychologists, but rather with what he himself considered to be the perfectly sound point of departure of all of their arguments: with the major premises of all four paralogisms. In these premises, Kant tells us repeatedly already in the first edition of the chapter on the Paralogisms, we come up with nothing more than trivial, merely analytic judgments about our selves. He explains further in a "general remark" (*CPR* B406) preceding the second edition of the Paralogisms that the major premises of all four paralogisms are statements made about the empty and indeterminate form "I think"; and it is on account of that circumstance that these statements are *themselves* empty and tautological.

But while this is how Kant characterizes both his procedure in arriving at the four major premises of the paralogisms and the status of those premises themselves, his claims on both issues are open to challenge. I am thinking here of—and anticipating—the main criticism that Hegel will soon address, in this connection, against Kant's position. In the first place, then, while it may be the case that the major premise in every paralogism is indeed a trivial (analytic) truth, it is not trivially true that there are, and we are in possession of, several of those trivial truths; it is not trivially true that these truths are such as they are and not any other, that they stand in such and such reciprocal relations and so on. The "empty I" is not *entirely* empty after all: it clearly exhibits certain aspects and relations which we can, somehow, grasp. Given all this, we must note, in the second place, that the circular and self-referential feature of the representing "I" is not, after all, an insurmountable obstacle to our achievement of some cognitive access to the "I" itself. And since we do gain some knowledge of the representing "I" *in spite of* the latter's circular and self-referential feature, we may as well reflect on the conditions of the possibility of this accomplishment of ours and we will then, perhaps, come to see that what has occurred forces us to take another look at the nature of the self and at the nature of self-knowledge; and we may thus find ourselves on our way to formulate a theory capable of supplying an intelligible account of those new data about the self and our knowledge of it. It will be Hegel's own ambition to supply precisely such a theory.

It is important, then, to consider in some detail how our grasp of the mere form "I think" as the condition of possibility of all representations yields the four "analytic propositions" (*CPR* B407–9) that make up the major premises in the four paralogisms.

In the first paralogism—of substantiality—this connection is quite transparent (*CPR* A349–50). No representation can be entertained by me without it being considered *my* representation. But insofar as representations are thus considered as belonging to me, I must consider myself as their "bearer" or their "owner"—and that means precisely as a *substance* in which they all inhere. The category of substance, of course, is not to be used here—as it will be by the rational psychologist—in its schematized form, adapted to the application to empirical objects. For the "I" thought of as the bearer of all representations is not a candidate for becoming an object of experience; and so the category of substance which we here apply to the "I" must remain a mere logical form. As such a logical form, however, the category can be employed to at least "think"[49] the formal relationship between the "I" and its representations.

In the second paralogism—of simplicity—the major premise is taken up by the rational psychologist as the stepping stone for the proof of the immortality of the soul. Viewed correctly, however, the premise is an analytic proposition grounded in our grasp of the "I think" as the form of all representations (*CPR* A355). The representing "I," we remember, must be thought of as absolutely empty. Any complexity and manifoldness in our conception of the "I" would mean that we are dealing with the *determinable* self—that is, with the self viewed as a particular represented item and not as the form in which all items are to be represented. Now, that absolute emptiness of the representing (the *determining*) self is absolute simplicity: "*'I am simple'* means nothing more than that this representation, 'I', does not contain in itself the least manifoldness and that it is absolute (although merely logical) unity" (*CPR* A355). The "absolute (although merely logical) unity" that Kant mentions in the last part of the sentence is the sort of unity that representations can acquire only because of their being entertained by a simple self. This is still another—an indirect—way in which Kant proves the simplicity of the representing self. To use Kant's own example (*CPR* A352): were we to distribute among several persons several different parts (words, thoughts, etc.) of one and the same verse, we would have representations of several different and unrelated thoughts, but we would not have the representation of one complete thought making up the verse. For such one complete thought (or the verse as a whole) to be possible, all of its parts must be entertained within the *unity* of one simple self. By analyzing this example Kant shows, further, how the simplicity of the self is in turn the condition of the possibility of the very unity of the representations in a self. In effect, if the self that entertains the manifold of representations were itself to be manifold, then its own manifoldness in turn could not exhibit any unity without being entertained by one simple self. Thus the self that entertains the manifold of representations must itself be represented as void of any manifoldness. But this emptiness of the representing self is nothing other, we recall, than the self's simplicity. And so in order to bring the manifold of representations to its required unity, the self must be simple. To sum up: whether we start directly from the representation "I think" or indirectly from the unity of all other representations, the representing self turns up as void of any determinateness and that means also as absolutely simple.

In the major premise of the third paralogism the numerical identity of the self at different times is correctly posited as a feature of the "I think" and this feature is then incorrectly inflated by the rational psychologist. Let us put Kant's point in the first person. In my representation of different times (say t, t', t'', etc), my "I" must be thought of as numerically identical (throughout t, t', t'', etc.), for these different times are all represented by *me* "and it comes to the same whether I say that this whole time is in me, an individual unity, or that I am to be found as numerically identical in all this time" (*CPR* A362). Apart from its special focus on time, the argument is indistinguishable from Kant's exploration in the second paralogism of the "absolute unity" of representations in a self. Moreover, in the second edition of the *Critique* the third paralogism is cast in quite general terms: the identity of my "I" is said to be implied by my awareness of "all the manifold of which I am conscious" (*CPR* B408); and thus my numerical identity at different times is simply a special case of that "analytic unity of consciousness" that Kant was expounding on as far back as the Transcendental Deduction.

The fourth paralogism is concerned mainly with supplying the grounds for a refutation of skepticism about the existence of the external world. Already in an earlier section titled Refutation of Idealism, and in a long footnote attached to the preface of the second edition of the *Critique,* Kant has made significant moves towards that goal. In both of these texts Kant tried to show how our empirical consciousness, qua temporal, implies directly and without any inference the existence of independent objects in space. Now, while these objects are indeed independent of our empirical consciousness, they are not independent of the transcendental self. Here lies the faulty assumption of the rational psychologist: he first assumes that those independent objects ought to be viewed as things in themselves (i.e., as altogether independent of the self) and he then draws, quite validly, his skeptical conclusion concerning their existence and our knowledge of them.

In the second edition of the chapter on Paralogisms all of this is greatly simplified. The argument itself does not proceed from the temporal status of my representations but—as in all other paralogisms—merely from my *existence* as a thinking "I":[50] "That I distinguish my own existence as that of a thinking being, from other things outside me—among them my body— is likewise an analytic proposition; for *other* things are such as I think to be *distinct* from myself" (*CPR* B409). Insofar, then, as *I* am, something other than myself must be too—something that is *not* me. The "I," that is, is a *polar concept*: its application demands the application of the concept of "non-I."[51]

The Kantian treatment of rational psychology represents, from Hegel's point of view, a wrong solution to the problems generated by a wrong approach. The rational psychologist's approach is wrong for it is carried out within a conceptual framework imposed by abstract understanding (*Verstand*)—the predictable result being the thing-like, reified view of the self the rational psychologist finds himself saddled with. The inconsistencies and the unsupported claims of rational psychology are then a foregone conclusion. But the Kantian solution offers no hope of progress either. While Kant fully—and correctly—realized that the categories of *Verstand* can be of no use to us in formulating any valid metaphysical claims about the self, his refusal to search for new ways to conceptually grasp the ultimate nature of the self, and his consistent reduction of the "I" to a merely formal logical function, do not add up to much progress over Hume's skepticism (*SL* 777).

Hegel's criticisms of both Kant and rational psychology presuppose the intelligibility and the truth of an entirely different approach to the life of the mind: of Hegel's own approach. For if there is no sound alternative to those "abstract" categories of *Verstand* that Hegel so vehemently condemns, then his criticisms can at best be viewed as expressions of intellectual frustration and uneasiness; but they most certainly cannot be viewed as stepping stones on a journey towards a more satisfy-

ing solution of the problematic of the self. We will, in the next
chapter, take a close look at the very foundation of what Hegel
thought that satisfying solution is and ought to be. For the time
being we can do no more than barely sketch out the path that
Hegel will take in moving beyond rational psychology and the
Kantian solution to its paralogisms.

Hegel himself returns to this general theme in several
places.[52] His overall assessment of the rational psychologists'
positions seems at first to represent something of a paradox: The
metaphysicians of the soul are accused, if not of an outright
empiricism, then at least of the fault of employing "the *general
idea* of spirit taken from empirical *consciousness*" (*SL* 773). But
the paradox—an accusation of empiricism thrown at, of all
people, the metaphysicians!—is more apparent than real. It is
true, of course, that the metaphysics of the soul is not an empirical science. And yet this metaphysics does not advance a
single step beyond the conception of the self that guides the
empirical study of mind. In both cases—of empirical psychology and of rationalistic metaphysics—the self is viewed as an
object among other objects, as a "soul-thing" (*Enc.* III, #378,
Zusatz) endowed with fixed and stable properties; most of these
can be discovered by empirical observation while some may call
for a purely rational inquiry by a metaphysician. Because the self
as investigated *both* by empirical and rational psychology is a
thing-like, reified item in which the determinations of spirit—
spirit's unity and multiplicity, its simplicity and manifoldness,
etc.—exist in sharply separated forms, any philosophical theory
of the self allied with those investigations will find itself committed to, and unable to decide between, the incompatible, conflicting views of the nature of the self: since the "essence [of spirit] is
constituted by the absolute unity of opposition in the *Notion*, it
exhibits in its phenomenal aspect and relation to externality
[i.e., as viewed by the metaphysics of the soul] contradiction in
its extreme form. Consequently, it must be possible to adduce
an experience in support of each of the opposed reflective determinations, or starting from experience it must be possible to
arrive at opposite determinations by way of formal syllogistic
reasoning" (*SL* 776). Thus, Hume's claim that no impression of
the self is to be found anywhere in our mental life can easily be
opposed by someone claiming that his own introspection sup-

plies him with entirely different *empirical* data. And, again, a *metaphysical* argument in favor of the substantiality or simplicity of the soul can easily be countered with a metaphysical argument justifying the opposite view.

In diagnosing and disposing of the inflated metaphysical claims generating the four paralogisms of rational psychology Kant did not question the rational psychologists' basic assumption: he did not cast any doubt upon the fixed and abstract *Verstand*-categories employed by the metaphysicians of the soul. What he did was merely to restrict the use of those categories by stripping them of any reference to the order of things—and hence also of any reference to the ultimate nature of ourselves. For, Kant argued, any valid employment of the categories presupposes their connection with intuition; and as the thinking self cannot be exhibited in any intuition, no substantive claims about the nature of that self can be justified. We can, of course, advance and test a host of claims concerning the empirical self; but then this ("determinable") self is not the ("determining") self whose nature was discovered through the argument of the metaphysicians. Of the former self we have knowledge as good as that of any other object of experience; of the latter self we know nothing at all. As Hegel puts it in his summary of Kant's final conclusion: "by this 'I', or if you like, *it* (the thing) that thinks, nothing further is represented than a transcendental subject of thoughts = x" (*SL* 776).

The reason why we cannot exhibit the determining self in any intuition is due, we recall, to that "circular" and self-referential status of the self in question. Insofar as each and every content that is to be entertained by me must be represented by my "I," the "I" itself cannot be made into a represented item. For Kant, this circumstance is the decisive obstacle in the way of any nonempirical self-knowledge. For Hegel, however, this "inconvenience"—the expression is Kant's and Hegel uses it mockingly—should rather be seen as a tremendous advantage in precisely the same respect.

In effect, Hegel argues, due to its circular structure the self exists *for itself* and it is thus capable of grasping itself in its multifarious aspects and activities. If Kant thought otherwise, it is because he—like the rational psychologists he criticized—employed the ordinary, commonsensical categories of *Verstand*;

but with the aid of *those* categories the unity of the self cannot be grasped as passing over into manifoldness, and so the "I" must remain entirely empty: "If 'I' is taken not in its Notion, but as a mere, simple, general idea, in the way we pronounce 'I' in every-day consciousness, then it is the abstract determination and not the self-relation that has itself for object. In that case, it is only *one* of the extremes, a one-sided subject without its objectivity" (*SL* 778). On the other hand, if we are willing—and capable—of abandoning the fixed categories of *Verstand,* then the "I" will turn up as manifesting itself in a rich multiplicity of its aspects. Some of these aspects—the functions of judging as well as the qualities that the thinking "I" is led to ascribe to itself in its capacity of the ultimate subject of judgments—were discovered by Kant himself; however poor his conception of the self might have been, it did have some content after all, and it did give us some insight into the "I" qua representing. The lack of sensible intuition in which to exhibit the pure self has not proved to be an obstacle to our achievement of that (however modest) knowledge of that self; and, in any case, the objection that the pure self cannot be exhibited in our ordinary sensible intuition is no objection at all: "If external intuition, determined in space and time, is required for objectivity, and it is this that is missing here, then it is quite clear that by objectivity is meant merely sensuous reality; and to have risen above *that* is a condition of thinking and of truth" (*SL* 778).

Everything, then, hinges upon Hegel's ability to deliver on his promise of presenting us with a mode of comprehension where the antinomies and the false alternatives generated by our reliance upon the ordinary sensible intuition, on the one hand, and upon the abstract categories of ordinary understanding, on the other hand, could indeed be overcome. Unless we are presented with such a new mode of comprehension, we have no choice but to opt either for the metaphysics of the soul or for Kant's critical philosophy—and yet neither of these two positions can be satisfying. The metaphysicians' advantage over Kant is clear—they, at least, aim at the knowledge of things as they really are, they aim at *truth*. If, in Kant, we avoid the pitfalls to which this metaphysics must ultimately lead, we do it at the price of abandoning the search for truth and of drifting into a form of skepticism—a skepticism which is not free of inconsistencies either, since the conflicting and irreconcilable claims that the pre-critical metaphysics made about the nature of things are now shifted to, and reemerge within, the system of our knowledge.[53]

In concluding his general criticism of both Kant and rational psychology, Hegel contrasts his adversaries' fixed and one-sided notions of the self with his own conception of "consciousness" (*Bewusstsein*): "In this form the free Notion, as *ego that is for itself*, is withdrawn from objectivity, but relates itself to it as *its other*" (*SL* 781). Here the self is not a fixed, thing-like entity—or else an empty, lifeless form of the Kantian "I think"—but a movement of setting itself in differences (in "its other") without losing thereby its enduring and continuing identity. It must be said at once that *Bewusstsein* represents this life of spirit in a very poor and still underdeveloped form. But then *Bewusstsein* itself does not exist autonomously; as Hegel repeats and argues tirelessly,[54] the "truth" of consciousness is to be found in self-consciousness (*Selbstbewusstsein*). In other words, consciousness exists only as a moment of self-consciousness; and it is only with self-consciousness that we enter "the native land of truth"[55] where the destiny of the self—to preserve its identity in all the richness and variety of its otherness—becomes a realized, actual fact of the life of spirit. Now self-consciousness *can* emerge as an actual, realized fact only by (first) opposing itself and (then) finding itself in another self-consciousness. The moment of opposition—the stance through which the self distinguishes itself from other selves, gains a separate identity and *endures* in that separation—is realized in a *life-and-death struggle* of the selves-.[56] Violence—*human* violence—and the ability to endure one's exposure to violence lie at the foundation of man's ascent to the level of self-consciousness.

In the *Science of Logic*—the centerpiece of Hegel's system—self-consciousness is conceptualized with the aid of the logical category of Being-for-self (*Für-sich-sein*). A close study of that category—of its meaning, its emergence, and its function in Hegel's *Logic*—will thus allow us to grasp and to assess at its most fundamental level Hegel's understanding of violence.

II.   HEGEL: LOGOS AND VIOLENCE

To be thus self related in the passage, and in the other, is the
genuine Infinity. . . . Thus Being, but as negation of the negation, is
restored again: it is now *Being-for-self.* . . . The *fundamental notion
of philosophy* [is] the genuine infinite. (*Enc.* I, #95, pp. 139-40; my
emphasis)

The statements with which we have concluded the last section of
our first chapter are open to an immediate challenge. We have
pointed out the role of violence in the emergence of human self-
consciousness as seen by Hegel; we then suggested that the
proper terrain for our investigation of the role of violence in
Hegel will be not his *Phenomenology of Spirit* but the *Science of
Logic.* And this suggestion seems to be entirely off-target, since
Hegel's *Logic* is concerned not with this or that aspect of man's
formative experience but with the structure and the development of *pure thinking.*

Against this important objection at least two replies can be
tried out.

1. In the very Introduction to his *Greater Logic* Hegel points
out (*SL* 48) that the *Phenomenology* serves as the justification—
indeed as the *only* justification there is—of the philosophical
stance adopted and pursued by the *Science of Logic.* The standpoint of the *Science of Logic* is said to be "deduced" (*SL* 49) in the
Phenomenology, and what this "deduction" consists in is spelled
out by Hegel in quite specific terms. The *Phenomenology* follows
up the unfolding and the growth of human experience, where
the term "experience" (*Erfahrung*) is to be understood in the
broadest possible sense, encompassing the cognitive, but also
the moral, the political, and so on, experiences of man. All of
these experiences are defined by some form of opposition between the experiencing self (the "subject") and the experienced
reality (the "object"); but all of these experiences lead up to and
culminate in the stage of Absolute Knowledge where the opposition in question abolishes itself and where the categories
governing the thinking of a human self show themselves to be
embedded in being (ibid.). It is precisely with this assumption
of the accomplished unity of thought and being that the *Science*

of Logic begins; and, for this reason, the *Phenomenology* is needed
to "justify" and to "deduce" the *Logic*.

Now, since Hegel's *Logic* seems to presuppose his *Phenomenology* and since the *Phenomenology* is concerned with nothing
other than the exploration of human experience in all of its
multifarious forms and shapes, one can argue that, precisely for
this reason, a conception and an account of human experience
must precede and condition the *Science of Logic*.

Unfortunately, this reply creates more problems than it
solves. For while the *Phenomenology* is said to be the "justification" and the "deduction" of *Logic*—and hence also of Hegel's
system as a whole, since Hegel's analyses of social and natural
worlds are conducted with the aid of a conceptual grid laid out
in the *Science of Logic*—it can also be shown that the *Phenomenology* itself is, and can be, nothing more than a part of Hegel's
system, a part subordinated to, and dependent upon, the very
same *Science of Logic* it was meant to "justify" in the first place.
This difficulty is well known to Hegel scholarship as the problem of an "introduction" to Hegel's system.[1] Even the external
organization of the system—in the *Encyclopaedia of the Philosophical Sciences*—is a testimony to the seriousness of the difficulty.
For the *Encyclopaedia* begins with a compressed version of
Hegel's *Logic* while the similar version of the *Phenomenology* is
situated in the very last volume of the *Encyclopaedia*, dealing
with the *Philosophy of Mind* in general. Far from being the justification and the deduction of *Logic*, the *Phenomenology* is
dramatically cut down in size to the status of a mere part of the
system as a whole.

Neither is it the case that this subordination of the *Phenomenology* to *Logic* is due to Hegel's desire to organize his system in a
simplified form for the benefit of his readers and his students.
Such a subordination of the first work to the second seems to be
required by the subject matter at hand. In the very same text—in
the Introduction to the *Greater Logic*—where Hegel was telling
us about that "justification" and "deduction" of his *Logic* by his
Phenomenology, he also tells us (*SL* 53) that the latter represents a
mere "example" of a method whose meaning and exposition can
be brought out only within the former. But if the method with
the aid of which the experiences of consciousness are conceptualized in the *Phenomenology* is, in the last analysis, dependent

upon the insights achieved within the *Science of Logic*, then the *Phenomenology* can in no sense be considered the *justification* of *Logic*. And it then seems that the objection we have raised against the concluding statements of our Chapter I remains perfectly valid: no understanding of human experience (and hence also no understanding of the human experience of violence) is needed to secure the intelligibility of Hegel's *Logic*.

2. There is another line of reply still open to us. It is Hegel's claim[2] that the *Phenomenology* and the *Science of Logic* are, in a sense, strictly parallel: the very same concepts that emerge in the *Phenomenology* will exhibit themselves, in the very same order, in the element of pure thinking as the latter is studied in the *Science of Logic*. But if such is the case, then one may well try to argue that a logical category is simply the atemporal skeleton of an experiential stage of human consciousness; and so the understanding of such an experiential stage must guide and condition our grasp of the corresponding logical category.

But this is not a valid reply either. In the first place, the correspondence between the categorial development of the *Science of Logic* and the experiential development in the *Phenomenology of Spirit* does not exhibit any rigorous isomorphism; there are many stages where the correspondence between the logical and the experiential development cannot be established. In the second place—and much more importantly—from the fact that the logical categories are also embedded in human experiences it does not yet follow that our understanding of those categories qua logical must depend upon our understanding of them qua experienced. To be sure, this *may* still turn out to be the case; but there is nothing that would allow us to decide beforehand that such *must* be the case.

In the analyses that follow I shall choose a different way of dealing with our difficulty and, in doing so, I shall be adopting Hegel's own way of approaching philosophical problems. For the moment, I shall put aside the question of method I have raised at the beginning of the chapter and I shall undertake a detailed study of Hegel's own moves in the *Science of Logic*, beginning with the great triad Being-Nothing-Becoming. For if it turns out that the logical development *itself* refers us, for its own intelligibility and truth, to some underlying paradigms found only in human experiences, then we will have every right to conclude that the Hegelian Logos as a whole is indeed shot through with an *anthropological content*. Should this possibility materialize in the course of our forthcoming analyses we will be in a position to see if and how that anthropological content of *Logic* includes the experience of human violence and of man's exposure to a violent world.

We must, therefore, begin directly with the purely logical beginning—with the very point of departure of Hegel's *Science of Logic*.

I.   Being

But the idea of this logical beginning presents us at once with the following paradox. In order to investigate the pure Logos (the unity of pure being and pure knowledge) in its own inner unfolding and intelligibility we must, in the first place, put aside our own presuppositions and assumptions. Instead of imposing upon the subject matter at hand our own biases, we ought "simply to take up *what is there before us*" (*SL* 69). Now if our own reflections upon and interpretations of the material we study—of *any* such material and thus also of the pure Logos as it is to be studied in the *Science of Logic*—amount to the process of mediating that material, then it follows that the *Logic's* point of departure ought to be the unity of thought and being in its *"simple immediacy"* (ibid.). This, again, must be understood in the two senses corresponding to the two sides of the logical beginning. Since the latter includes both the pure being and the pure knowledge, (ibid.) we must start with what is at once the first determination of being and the first stage of the conceptual structure of our knowledge.

The paradox of the logical beginning can now be spelled out. On the one hand, we must begin our philosophizing with a purely passive cognitive attitude: we must let go our own biases and preconceptions in order to be able to grasp "what is simply there"—the *Logos* in its "simple immediacy." But—and here is the rub—that immediacy is not *itself* immediately given and "simply there," spread in front of our intellectual gaze, as it were. On the contrary, as Hegel points out, this simple immediacy is the result of our own efforts to distinguish it from what is already mediated: "Simple immediacy is itself an expression of reflection and contains a reference to its distinction from what is mediated" (ibid.). As it turns out, then, the logical beginning *is* mediated after all: in its desired pristine purity it can only be reached after we have distilled it from the distortions and biases of all the forms of mediated thinking. For the same reason, the beginning seems to be a "result" even when taken in the element of pure thinking (i.e., independently of the *Phenomenology of Spirit*). As it turns out, not only do we have to liberate the categories of pure thought from their embodiment in nature and history, but, in addition, the separation of the immediacy of *Logos* itself from its more mediated forms is the end result of a strenuous exercise of an intellectual skill in sorting out the pure concepts. The task before us, then, seems to involve a contradiction in terms: we are told to take in, as it were, "what is simply there before us" while at the same time being fully responsible for putting it there in the first place.

However, the difficulty is not insurmountable. We do make a presupposition, but it is a second-order presupposition to purify our thinking of its presuppositions. *Our* presupposition is nothing other than the decision to philosophize: if the philosophical enterprise is to make sense, then, its first step, inevitably, ought to be to purge our thought of all kinds of naive and untested beliefs which we take for granted. In this respect the logical beginning is —or at least ought to be—the very opposite of the phenomenological beginning. While the *Phenomenology* takes, as its point of departure, the *pre*-philosophical, "natural" consciousness, the *Science of Logic* is nothing else but the articulation of our ultimate *philosophical* comprehension of reality. As long as we are prepared to recognize the legitimacy of such an enterprise in general, we must be prepared to accept its traditional aim to rid our thought of all naively accepted beliefs and conceptions. At the same time, Hegel is fully aware that such an aim cannot be achieved until the *Science of Logic* has reached its completion. The soundness of our point of departure (in the great triad Being-Nothing-Becoming) will prove its worth to philosophy insofar as it will show itself to be the ground of all the other logical categories—of all the categories, that is, that are of concern to philosophical speculation. As we make our way through the *Science of Logic* we notice that "the beginning of

philosophy is the *foundation* which is present and preserved
throughout the entire subsequent development" (*SL* 71; my
emphasis). And this sort of justification for the beginning to be
chosen cannot be decided by any a priori investigation concerning the "method" of the philosophical inquiry, but only by our
success in actually doing philosophy.[3]

We can understand now why the concept of *pure being* as
defined at the dawn of philosophy by Parmenides (*SL* 83) must
be taken as the logical beginning. Since the latter must be "absolute," "it *may not presuppose anything*" (*SL* 70). Its only
quality, therefore, must be "pure indeterminateness" (*SL* 72);
every specific, determinate conception of being already takes for
granted the validity of this or that concept it inevitably employs.
But the philosophical beginning must be the suspension of all
such merely taken-for-granted, untested thoughts and conceptions. To begin philosophizing means, for Hegel, to assert the
total autonomy of thought. We must take the pure being as our
point of departure, for only the pure being is the "unity into
which the pure knowing *withdraws*" (*SL* 72; my emphasis). This
"withdrawal" from and suspension of all the specific conceptions and determinations of being is indeed a presupposition we
adopt—but it is the sort of presupposition without which philosophy as such would be meaningless.

We must avoid the danger of confusing the pure being's total
indeterminateness with the (alleged) universal extension of the
concept of being. From the vantage point of the Parmenides-
Hegel "beginning," the concept of pure being does not refer to
objects qua particular entities—trees, houses, and the like. To
be sure Hegel, unlike Parmenides, does not, therefore, relegate
particular entities to the realm of nonbeing. Still, taken merely
as the articulation of the stage where our philosophical thought
must begin, Hegel's description of pure being corresponds to
Parmenides'.[4]

But—one could now object—if the starting point of philosophy must be free of any presuppositions, what right do we
have to presuppose being itself? If a fully indeterminate conception is to be our only secure point of departure, why should we
inject into that conception some additional complexity by making it a conception of an indeterminate *being*?

The question needs to be raised, but the answer is obvious: the separation of being and truth, if valid at all, is absent at the beginning stage of philosophical thinking. At first, being and truth belong to the same family of notions.[5] To doubt that we are legitimate in talking about things as they *truly are* amounts to saying that we doubt the legitimacy of the very concept of truth. Philosophy can not begin with such a doubt. Even while we suspend our assent to all particular determinations of being, we cannot suspend our assent to being and truth in general. More than that: our suspension of the former is sustained *precisely* by our commitment to the latter—we have decided to carry out the "withdrawal" of thought from all specific determinations in order not to distort our conception of being.

Something now needs to be said about the division of the logic of Being in general (*SL* 79–80). This part of Objective Logic is divided into three sections which deal with Being as Quality, as Quantity (which is Quality sublated), and as Measure (the unity of Quality and Quantity). The precise meaning and the interrelationships of these categories will be established in the course of the logical dialectic of Being. The only specific point Hegel brings out at this stage is his reason for the priority of Quality over Quantity—and even this point cannot be fully grasped until we have covered the appropriate stages and transitions within the general category of Being. However, some grounds can be given to this choice even now (ibid.) We have already seen that what constitutes the logical beginning can be nothing other than pure being—being in its simplest, unmediated determination. But quantity is tantamount to the injection of mediation into our grasp of being, for quantity is, in effect, a levelling down, a homogenizing of quality. For example, by ascribing magnitude to qualitatively different items we can bring them to a common denominator, we can establish their numerical equivalences, etc. Nothing of this sort ought to be smuggled into our first conception of being.

It would seem, though, that were we to follow conscientiously Hegel's advice, our pure Being would end up by being stripped of any qualitative differentiation as well. For what is pure Being if it is only something that is *not* a mountain, a tree, a house, etc.? By asking this very question we have, however, already produced the required answer. Since we have set those determinate beings "in contrast to being in general" we have, implicitly, attributed a quality to pure being: the quality of indeterminateness (*SL* 81).

How are we to grasp this quality, though? Our attempt to do so yields the first transition in the *Science of Logic:* all of a sudden, pure being is turning into nothing. It is said often enough by Hegel himself and mechanically repeated by many, that pure being shows itself identical with pure nothing due to the total emptiness of both concepts. We say pure being and, since we mean nothing determinate, we mean nothing at all, pure nothing. But then why is pure being still *different* from pure nothing? "It counts as a distinction whether something or *nothing* is intuited or thought" (*SL* 82). This could easily be granted if Hegel was here talking—as Plato did in the *Sophist*—about a *determinate* nothing or "non-being." But this is not, emphatically, what Hegel is here talking about.[6] On the contrary, the presence of a determinate nothing in our acts of thought is due to the nothing in general. How, then, do we make sense of the *difference* between the original "undifferentiatedness" insofar as it is called *being* and the same "undifferentiatedness" (*SL* 82 insofar as it is called *nothing*? Both expressions ("being" and "nothing") refer not to the "that" but to the "what" of whatever it is that we are thinking at the beginning of *Logic*. Both expressions, that is, refer precisely to the quality of what is thought at the beginning. But this quality is differentiated into being and nothing; and (*SL* 83) the nothing is real to us (it *is;* it has a "that") precisely because we think nothing as meaning something *different* from being (i.e., as having a different "what" than being has). If we don't want to explain away that difference as due to a confused way of thinking we must give it some content. But then again: to give the difference a content (*any* content, it seems) would be possible only if we were talking about *determinate* being and nothing. It is not permissible to fall back, at this stage, upon Hegel's own later statements (*SL* 92) to the effect that the implied difference between being and nothing is "unsayable" (*unsagbar*), as long as both being and nothing are not viewed as aspects of becoming. For the reason why becoming will have emerged in the first place is that we were confronted with both identity *and* difference of being and of nothing.

In the end, in order to illuminate the meaning of that initial difference between being and nothing, Hegel appeals to a *paradigm of the human condition*. The philosophical inquiry begins with a focus on what is posited unconditionally and without any presuppositions: the "absolute" (*SL* 70) of pure being. But in holding onto those "absolute riches" (*Enc.* I, #87, Zusatz)—the riches the possession of which is not dependent upon anything else—we end up with an "absolute poverty" (ibid.). Being slips through our fingers and we are left with nothing. To say that only being as such—and not this or that particular bĕing—belongs to you amounts to saying that nothing is truly yours. Conversely, too, if you become indifferent to each and all of your particular ties and attachments you may still claim that the world "as such" is your proper domain: what is yours is yours absolutely and unconditionally, since it cannot be taken away from you under any circumstances. Is it then to be wondered that the Nothing is the principle of Buddhism (*SL* 83), with its underlying *human attitude* of making oneself indifferent to the vicissitudes of life? Now we can see that elusive difference between pure being and pure nothing: to the man dazzled by the *absolute riches* of pure being it does not occur that he is, in fact, *utterly destitute*. But this is precisely what will occur to him when he thinks about the worth of these riches. He will then realize that he has nothing to call his own and that, in effect, pure being and pure nothing are identical. Insofar, then, as riches are simply riches, they are not poverty (pure being is not pure nothing). But insofar as riches are absolute riches, they are indistinguishable from pure nothing.

We are now certain to hear the objection that our talk about man's "indifference" to the conditions of his life is inappropriate within a purely logical study. Yet these are the very same terms that Hegel himself uses both in the *Greater Logic* and in the first part of his *Encyclopaedia*. And it is clear from what he there says that such an *attitude of indifference* is indeed constitutive for one's ability to properly grasp the relationship of pure being and pure nothing:

If Being and Nought (*Nichts*) are identical, say these objectors, it follows, that it makes no difference whether my home, my property, the air I breathe, this city, the sun, the law, mind, god, are or are not. . . .

[but] the teaching of philosophy is precisely what frees man from the
endless crowd of finite aims and intentions, by making him so insensi-
ble (*gleichgültig*) to them that their existence or non-existence is to him
a matter of indifference (*Enc.* I, #88).

Man has a duty to rise to that abstract universality of *mood* (*Gesinnung*) in which he is indeed indifferent (*gleichgültig*) to the existence or
non-existence of the hundred dollars . . . just as it ought to be a matter
of indifference (*gleichgültig*) to him whether he is or is not" (*SL* 89; my
emphasis).

A rich harvest can be gathered from a closer analysis of these
passages. The example of a hundred thalers is, of course, Kant's
(*CPR* A599, B627). Against Kant's famous dictum "being is
not a real predicate of the thing" Hegel will first point out that in
our *commonsensical* understanding of existence and nonexistence
these two terms are by all means the "real predicates" of the
thing; or, to put it differently, it is not at all the case—contrary
to what Kant thought—that existence and nonexistence are not
the determinations of a thing's content. In effect, given the
ordinary, commonsensical attitude, the real and the unreal hundred dollars will differ profoundly in their relations (and hence
also in qualities, since a quality cannot be defined independently
of its relations with other qualities). Their very content will thus
differ, for "it is a content standing in a necessary relation to
another content, to the whole world" (*SL* 86). Those hundred
dollars' "being," we may say, is *constituted* by their relations and
connections with the fabric of the world: I believe that the
hundred dollars I think I have in my pocket are real because they
have some visible and tangible impact upon the state of my
fortune (*SL* 85); I discover their reality insofar as—and only to
the extent that—the option of going to a fancy restaurant or of
buying myself a pair of fashionable shoes becomes open to me.
If the hundred dollars at issue are not envisioned as having some
such tangible and visible impact, their very content changes
rapidly—and so too does my ordinary notion of them. How
was it possible, for Kant, to have so drastically misread these
ordinary notions? His mistake was to have considered the hundred dollars "*in isolation*" (*SL* 88). For if I cannot identify any
concrete impact the being or the nonbeing of the hundred dollars would have upon me, then their existence or the absence of
it become indeed a matter of indifference to me—they leave me

cold, as it were—and I am then prepared to hold that being is not a real predicate of the thing or that being is not a determination of the thing's "content." Within the plain, ordinary attitude I may, of course, lack any narrowly practical interest in the existence or nonexistence of those hundred dollars; my attitude towards them may be that of a perceiver simply interested in finding out whether they are or are not items in the furniture of the world. But this does not invalidate Hegel's general point. For even in cases of the ordinary perceptual exploration, I ascribe existence and nonexistence to a thing only given my ability to establish some links between the thing in question and other things. If there is no trace of those hundred dollars in my bank account, or if my pocket does not show that familiar bulge, or if my friend tells me that the jacket I left at his house has nothing in its pockets, then I must begin to wonder if I really had that money to begin with. As J. L. Austin has shown[7]—unknowingly repeating Hegel—within the ordinary attitude our perceptual doubt is always entertained for specific reasons and it concerns a specific item or some specific items. The existence first doubted and then attributed or denied within such an attitude is thus a *determinate* existence and it therefore does differ in content from nonexistence.

With the focus upon the *indeterminate* being and nonbeing, their sharp difference begins to collapse. But the new focus demands a shifting away from the area of determinate existence (*SL* 89); and in order to accomplish such a shift the thinker must be, Hegel told us, in a special *Gesinnung* (mood, disposition, sentiment)—in the attitude of indifference towards the conditions of his life. The presence of this human attitude of indifference is not itself indifferent here; for unless this attitude provides the background and the context of our thinking, we will remain enclosed within the commonsensical categories of "understanding" (*Verstand*), holding fast to the abstract separation of being and nonbeing. Like all human attitudes, the mood of "indifference" is not, for Hegel, an inarticulate state of mind. It is a stance towards something and a stance taken in a certain meaningful way. It discloses the insignificance of one's life *as a whole;* to the man capable of rising to this mood it will not matter any more, Hegel told us, "whether he is or he is not"; and it is this awareness of one's finitude and perishability that—in

Hegel's words again—"frees the man from the endless crowd of finite aims and intentions." As long as we cannot think independently of the attachment to our life we will continue to cling to whatever it is that defines and sustains that life: home, country, the air that we breathe, and so on. And as long as we understand ourselves (as we do in the ordinary, everyday attitude) as defined by such items we shall continue to hold being and nonbeing apart from each other. Our entire ordinary way of life is predicated upon such a sharp distinction between being and nonbeing—above all in the case of our own being and then also, indirectly, in the case of the items making up our world. Conversely, the collapse of the ordinary attitude as a whole will make us free *from* our ties to determinate entities and free *for* our understanding of Being as such (pure being).

Our understanding of pure being and of its kinship with pure nothing bears the traces of the *Gesinnung* within which this understanding is achieved. Pure being, we remember, could be discovered only if we were prepared to rid ourselves of all of our "presuppositions"; if, that is, we were prepared to forgo all of our certainties and assumptions; if, in still other terms, we were prepared to take nothing for granted. But as long as I am unable to rise to the mood within which it makes no difference "whether I am or not," I remain confined to a way of life built on the foundation of at least some taken-for-granted conceptions and beliefs, including precisely that ordinary, commonsensical belief in the sharp distinction between being (if only in the case of *my* being) and nonbeing (if only in the case of *my* nonbeing, i.e., my death). In order to liberate my thought from its imprisonment within that distinction I must liberate the thinker—myself—from his inability to comprehend the finitude of his own condition. Thus the truly *philosophical* understanding of being and of nothing can be achieved only within man's mood of being aware of his own status as a finite creature.

The category of Becoming allows us to gain some further and more substantive clarifications of this philosophical understanding of being and nothing. Two points need to be made in this connection. First, the play of being and nothing yields the category of becoming (the latter is the result of that play). Second, our grasp of becoming supplies the framework within which we can articulate more sharply the identity-and-difference of being and nothing.

When considering pure being and pure nothing our thought found itself confronted with a *process*—with the mutual disappearing of being into nothing. This origination of nothing out of being and of being out of nothing is ordinarily represented as time (*SL* 84); but, Hegel adds immediately (*SL* 85), time (*Zeit*) gives a distorted image of becoming (*Werden*), since in time being and nonbeing are held apart (thus a democracy is simply destroyed by a tyranny that follows it in time, etc.). Elsewhere (*Enc.* II, ##257–59) Hegel will offer a detailed study of time as such an "*intuited* becoming" (ibid., #258), where different stages of a process are inevitably ascribed to merely different ("exclusive") slots in a temporal chronology. In contrast, in the logical category of pure *Werden* our thought is confronted with a *non*temporal becoming whose stages do not assume even a semblance of such an absolute, abstract difference.

But how are we to *understand* this strange notion of a non-temporal becoming of our thought?

Given the context of man's aspiration to anchor himself in the "absolute plenitude" (*Enc.* I, #87, Zusatz) of an unconditioned beginning, the passage of being into nothing loses at least some of its mystery. For those "absolute riches" of pure being have indeed slipped through our fingers and left us in the utter destitution of "absolute poverty." While this sequence must be thought independently of any temporal chronology—only thus can we avoid thinking, against Hegel's warnings,[8] that being first appears and only then passes over into nothing—we do gain some conception of such a peculiar slide from the expected riches of being to the rags of nothing we are left with. For in reaching out to unconditioned beginning our thought is set on a journey from an absolute plenitude and security to no plenitude and security—and hence to no plenitude and security at all. It is this going-back-and-forth between the two stations on our thought's journey that Hegel designates with the term "Becoming."[9]

Let us review again the two general points Hegel is here trying to make: becoming is both the result of the play of being and nothing and what allows us to articulate their proper relationship of identity-and-difference. Becoming is (1) the result of the play of being and of nothing since we found ourselves journeying from being to nothing due to our very attempt to think these two categories. Now (2) insofar as we think becom-

ing, we do think of starting out with something, and of this
something disappearing, going out of existence and turning
into nothing. And *this* category, Hegel thinks, is rich enough
and determinate enough to allow its conceptual articulation.

The two moments of becoming itself are generation and
decay, the coming-to-be and the ceasing-to-be. These two moments stand for, respectively, the passing over of being into
nothing and the passing over of nothing into being. Thus (*SL*
105) the two moments of becoming are themselves composed
of being and of nothing (arranged in opposite directions). We
start with being, with something, and what we start with slips
through our fingers, goes out of existence, becomes nothing:
this is the ceasing-to-be moment of becoming. We then start
with what is as yet nonexistent, with nothing, and we end up
with something, with being: this is the coming-to-be aspect of
becoming. And Hegel credits "the ancients" in general with the
discovery of origination and decay as the two "species of Becoming" (*Enc.* I, #89).

The two moments of becoming "paralyze" each other and
they thus reach a state of "equilibrium" (*SL* 106). Becoming
thus "settles" into a "stable result" (ibid.)—i.e., into a determinate being (*Dasein*). Determinate entities, we may say, are the
relatively stable and fixed items which result from, and endure
within, the constant flow of generation and decay. Here Aristotle's treatise *On Generation and Corruption* becomes highly
relevant as supplying the historical background of Hegel's analyses. Naturally—and quite unlike Aristotle in *On Generation
and Corruption*—we must study this "settling" of origination
and decay into a determinate being in a purely logical, speculative fashion. We ought not to guide ourselves by our perceptions but by a merely logical comprehension of the concepts of
coming-to-be and ceasing-to-be. "Although—Hegel tells us—
they [the coming-to-be and the ceasing-to-be] differ in direction they interpenetrate and paralyse each other" (*SL* 106).
When we think being we end up with nothing (decay), but
when we start with nothing we end up with being (origination).
And then this new being, in turn, passes over into nothing
(decay again). Another attempt, another return—this time
from decay to origination. Thus origination *is* decay and decay *is*
origination. At the same time, they are different as well, if only

in direction (from being to nothing or from nothing to being). The concept of a determinate being emerges in response to our attempts to think both the unity and the difference of origination and decay. Obviously—to put it in plain words—there is a difference between birth (origination) and death (decay). But then also everything that is born is always already on its way to die. We must now find a conception in which to articulate and to resolve this paradox.

What we need is the conception of something which is stable, but only relatively so. Without the conception of something stable (of something maintaining itself in being, at least for a while) we will not grasp the difference between origination and decay, between birth and death. But unless this something is only relatively—and not absolutely—stable, we will not understand the identity of origination and decay (we will miss the point about birth carrying in it the germ of death). Such a relatively stable something is inconceivable otherwise than as enclosed within certain limits. It must have an identity the destruction of which is its own (the something's) destruction. Such a something can only be *this*—but not that, or that, or something other again. We have arrived at a conception of a qualified being, a being with quality.

II.   Determinate Being

The chapter on Determinate Being begins with a section entitled "Determinate Being as Such." This section is itself divided into three subsections: (a) "Determinate Being in General"; (b) "Quality"; (c) "Something (Etwas)." Throughout the chapter Hegel analyzes the first appearance of a "paralyzed" and "stabilized" thinking—only to explode its stability and fixedness as the dialectic unfolding in the chapter gathers its momentum. The last section of the chapter is entitled "Infinity" and it both sums up and deepens the radical instability of determinate being. It turns out that *Dasein* was posited only to be transcended and surpassed. Moreover—and this too becomes clear as we make our way through the chapter—what undercuts the stability of determinate entities is what posited them to begin with: the becoming of thought. Our earlier interpretation of becoming allows us, therefore, to grasp the broader context within which the dialectic of determinate being and its supersession gain meaning. Our thought is set in the process of becoming insofar as it searches for the unconditioned and the presuppositionless: pure being escapes from our grip, leaving us with nothing, and this disappearance of being into nothing *is* becoming. Our thought is subjected to incessant unrest and movement due to that drive to reach the eluding Absolute. This drive, in turn, is made possible by a *mood,* or an *existential attitude,* in which man lets go of his attachment to life and becomes aware of the finitude of his condition. Therefore the supersession of determinate being in general (as due to becoming) is played out against the background of the thinker's sense of his own condition as a finite, mortal creature.

Determinate Being in General. Like Heidegger more than a hundred years later, Hegel will find it helpful to explore the etymology of *Dasein.* The term means, literally, being-there, and this "thereness," Hegel points out (*SL* 110), must not be confused with a spatial place. It stands only for the (merely logical) features of the determinate being. In effect, after the play of generation and decay has reached its equilibrium, being cannot be anything and everything: being has now acquired its own specific identity, its *determinateness (Bestimmtheit),* and the forthcoming stages of the dialectic will retrace the tension between being and its determinateness. But while both the pure being and the pure nothing are thus given a concrete, specific form in the notion of *Dasein,* they are also preserved in it (as they ought to be since, according to Hegel, all of the more concrete categories are, as it were, painted on the broad canvas of being and nothing in general). The following statement summarizes the present stage of logical dialectic: "Determinate being as the result of its becoming is, in general, being with a non-being such that this non-being is taken up into simple unity with being. *Non-being* thus taken up into being in such a way that the concrete whole is in the form of being, of immediacy, constitutes *determinateness as such*" (*SL* 110). But why call the determinateness of a being its *non*-being? The reason for this choice of words is as follows. When we take a being only qua being—i.e., only as a "bearer" of possible determinations—we consider it as still completely indeterminate, as a medium capable of receiving any attribute. And so when we ascribe to a being this or that determination we *negate* being: our attribution of some specific determination to a bearer is tantamount to exclusion of competing determinations (thus a thing cannot be red and green all over) and, therefore, it is tantamount to the negation of our bearer's initially unbounded possibilities to receive any and every determination. Thus, in Plato the undetermined *apeiron* gets both its determinateness and (hence) its limitation from the *peras*; in this capacity, the *peras* is the *negation* of the *apeiron*.[10]

The conception of a determinate being that we have reached so far is only immediate and therefore crude and oversimplified. Being and its determinateness are merely superimposed, brought together in a quite external fashion; their inner connection— much less the nature of that connection—has not yet been clarified or even touched upon (*SL* 110). It will not be brought out into the open until the separation of being and (its) determinateness will have been deepened and then brought to the breaking point. This takes us to the next stage of the dialectic of determinate being.

Quality. Suddenly, we are confronted with a significant shift in Hegel's terminology: instead of talking about determinateness, we find ourselves employing the much more restricted notion of *quality* (*Qualität*). There is no secret here, and Hegel anticipates and answers our question (*SL* 111). Determinateness is indeed a generic term which applies across the board to all kinds of attributes, but at our stage of conceiving bearers and attributes we are capable of forming the conception of only qualitative attributes. If—for example—we now wished to determine an item through the attribute of quantity, we would have to subsume the former under some universal scale of order and measurement. But the presently available conceptions are too poor to allow for such a complex operation. In fact (*SL* 114), we ought not even to confuse a quality with a property (*Eigenschaft*), for property is quality as already standing within the network of interactions with its environment: thus the property of bitterness is ascribed to an herb insofar as that herb has certain effects upon our sense of taste, etc. In contrast, quality is determinateness taken only immediately, i.e., in isolation. Naturally, one of Hegel's aims will be to show that such qualities are inherently unstable. In the end, it is not possible at all to consid-

er a determinate being (and hence its qualities) independently of
its relations to and interactions with other determinate beings.
But this will be the result, not the beginning, of the dialectic of
Dasein. In its first impulse our thought will focus precisely upon
an isolated *Dasein*—if only because nothing more was needed to
stabilize the process of generation and decay.

The stage of quality represents the extreme form of treating
Dasein in isolation. Not only are we considering an individual
entity, with all of its qualities, in isolation from its surroundings
but, in addition, we are even isolating those qualities themselves
from their bearer; we are viewing them as if they were not the
qualities *of* this particular entity.[11] Husserl will find later the
right terms for describing these two types of isolation. Due to
the first isolating move, we extract the thing's quality from the
thing's "outer horizon" (we consider the green color of that tall
aspen tree independently of the tree's natural setting in a mead-
ow, at the foot of a mountain, etc.). The second type of isolation
extracts the quality from its "inner horizon" (and so we try to
view this delicate light-green as if it did not belong to the tree at
all).

While the collapse of our strained attempt to isolate a quality
from its outer horizon will occur at a later stage, the impossibility of separating a quality from its own bearer (its inner
horizon, to continue with Husserl's terminology) dawns upon
us at once. In effect, we are quickly forced to draw the distinction *within* the isolated quality between (its) being and (its)
determinateness. And this distinction cannot sustain itself without rehabilitating—and in a strengthened form at that—the
very same link we were trying to deny: the link between a quality
and its bearer.

Let us focus again on that delicate light-greenness. On the
one hand, we are considering an item (color) with its own
specific content (green, delicate, etc.). On the other hand that
item—the quality—*is*. Quality, therefore, has within itself the
two aspects of being and determinateness, which are now called,
respectively, "reality" and "negation": "Quality taken in the
distinct character of *being*, is *reality;* as burdened with a negative
it is *negation* in general" (*SL* 111). And, again, in the *Encyclopaedia:* "Quality, as determinateness which *is*, as contrasted
with the Negation which is involved in it but distinguished

from it, is Reality" (*Enc.* I, #91). We are already familiar with
Hegel's rationale for identifying the aspect of determinateness
with "negation in general." This rule governs his present use of
terms as well. Insofar as the quality is not just any quality, but
this particular color, it contains the element of limitation, and
thus of negation of the open-ended determinateness of being.
The quality *is*, but its potential for being "anything and everything" is negated by its being the delicate green and not, for
example, a different kind of green. As Spinoza said, and as
Hegel reminds us here (*SL* 113; *Enc.* I. #91), *omnis determinatio
est negatio*. Thus, within the quality itself we discover at once the
play of being and of its negation. But this also means that the
isolation of quality from being—the opening move of our consideration of quality—cannot sustain itself. And if we persist in
isolating a quality from its bearer, then that quality, in turn,
becomes *itself* a bearer of further qualities. But then we may as
well face up to that inescapable law of thought and draw the
proper conclusion: "quality is completely unseparated from determinate being, which is simply determinate qualitative being"
(*SL* 115).

We have come full circle, but the presence of a new expression indicates that the result, although similar to the
beginning, is also richer than the latter. The being is not only—
as it was initially thought to be—a mere determinate being, but
a "determinate qualitative being." And this is due to the fact that
our vague conception of an individual bearer's determinateness
has now been replaced by a more concrete and more thought-
out conception of quality. We have first extracted determinateness from being (and we have thereby established the being's
determinateness in its status of a quality), we have then carefully
considered what it is like to be a quality, and we have finally been
led to the conclusion that this newly explored concept of quality
includes its necessary reference to a bearer. We thus have a more
concrete conception of the bearer itself, for we can now grasp it
as determined by something (the quality) the conception of
which has been enriched and rendered more detailed by the
entire movement of reflection and analysis which now lies behind us.

The "qualitative determinate being" is thus not a mere *Dasein*
anymore, but a "something" (*Etwas*). Its emergence is tanta-

mount to the first appearance of *negation of negation* and, in that
capacity, it represents the germ from which the Being-for-self
(*Für-sich-sein*) will ultimately spring (*SL* 115). The something is
a negation of negation insofar as the separatedness of the quality
and its bearer (this was the first negation: the quality was
thought as the negation, the constraint imposed upon the
bearer) could not be sustained and was in turn negated, or
rather it negated itself. The quality is now thought back *into* its
bearer; or rather, conversely, the bearer is thought as holding
onto its qualities as to *its own*. It rebels against our attempts to
extract them from it; and they, in turn, indicate to us that they
belong to their bearer. For this reason, "something (*Etwas*) is
the first *negation of negation,* as simple self-relation in the form of
being"; and hence our something is already "the beginning of
the subject [*Subjekt*]" (ibid.). Subjectivity, for Hegel, amounts
to an entity's ability to take up and to mold its own determinations. While there can be no question as yet of such a power to
mold and to shape one's own determinations (as will be the case
with the human self, capable of forming its own appetitions and
representations), we do see even now the sublation of a merely
external relation between a being and its qualities. They return
to it; they are posited as *its* qualities (the delicate greenness is
now the very special delicate greenness of an aspen tree; it is not
the delicate greenness of a sweater). Hegel wants us to talk here
about (a form of) "self-relation," for in relating itself to its
qualities, the bearer does not relate to something merely sup-
peradded upon it: it relates only to itself. It is *mediated*—
mediated by its qualities—but since those qualities are not foreign and indifferent to it (the delicate greenness of the aspen tree
is, for example, the beautiful and calm greenness of an aspen tree
and not the bland and plastic greenness of a sweater) it is mediated by itself; an elementary mode of "self-mediation" (*SL* 116)
has thus emerged.

But this simple (i.e., not thought-out, still merely given)
character of self-mediation present in the something will be the
reason of the something's undoing and of its passing over into
the next category. It is vital for our own interpretation of the
dialectic to pay close attention to Hegel's own commentary on
this passage. In effect, we are told not only that a merely given
form of self-relation is unsustainable, but we are also told in

advance just what it is that is still missing and what, therefore, will emerge as the completion of the immediate something. "Something *is,* and *is,* then also determinate being; further, it is *in itself* also *becoming*" (*SL* 116). "Something as a *becoming* is a transition, the moments of which are themselves somethings, so that the transition is *alteration*—a becoming which has already become *concrete*" (ibid.). We will not be able to fully understand the meaning of these statements until later (*SL* 128), when all the detailed stages of the something's career within the realm of the "Finitude" will have been covered. But Hegel's present talk about the inevitable subjection of something to becoming is highly significant for our entire interpretation of the dialectic. For if something is sublated by becoming and if becoming is— as we argued at the beginning—the unrest of a thought condi- tioned by man's mood of being fully aware of his own mortality, then the unfolding of the dialectic of something is, in effect, incomprehensible outside of an *existential attitude* of the thinker himself. It is an attitude in which the human individual's (the thinker's own) finitude and mortality are not trivialized and minimized by the reassuring "common sense" (*gesunde Men- schenverstand*). Thinking *within* this existential attitude, the thinker will, inevitably, refuse to accept any merely given and merely taken-for-granted conceptions. And since the something is just such a conception (for in the something the relation between being and quality is not yet systematically thought out but still, to a great extent, merely given) it will collapse under the scrutiny of a thought dissatisfied with any conceptual givenness and reaching out towards the unconditioned.

The relation of being and quality, albeit not totally external to its terms, is still so poor and so undeveloped that understand- ing succeeds easily in setting them apart once again. The understanding here at work is, quite specifically, the Kantian *Verstand.* This can be gathered not only from the sort of concep- tions that will gradually emerge in the course of the present section—entitled "Finitude" (*Endlichkeit*); we shall witness here the appearance and the dissolution of such characteristi- cally Kantian notions as the thing-in-itself (*Ding-an-sich*) and the ought (*Sollen*)—but, above all, from the general pattern of the dialectic in this whole section. We will observe here the workings of that reflective, abstract mode of thinking which holds fast to conceptual oppositions and differences. For example, being-in-itself will be set up as separated from being-for-other; the finite will be viewed as stripped of any connection with the infinite, and so on. Needless to say, this (merely) separating and dividing mode of thinking cannot survive a closer scrutiny conducted in conformity with its own standards and commitments.

We witness this self-abolition of *Verstand* from the very first subsection entitled "Something and an Other." Because of the poverty of the relation between being and quality in the something, we conceive that quality as the mere "other" (*Das Andere*) of the being of the something. The bearer qua existent and the bearer's quality are thus construed as two items brought together only by a "Third," i.e., by the external reflection of an observer who thinks about them and examines them (*SL* 118). The corresponding section of the *Encyclopaedia* gives a relatively clear indication of where we are: "Quality is Being-for-another—an expression of the mere point of Determinate being, or of something [*Etwas*]. The Being as such of quality, contrasted with this reference to something else, is Being-by-self" (*Enc.* I, #91). This passage sets up the general framework of the subsection, but the meanders of Hegel's dialectic are here much more detailed and complex. There are, in effect, three stages in the something's sharp division into its being and its quality.

"Something and other are, in the first place, both determinate beings or somethings" (*SL* 117). In other words, the determinateness of a something is *itself* construed as an independent entity set over against what was initially taken as its bearer. Hegel hints (*SL* 118) at Plato's *Sophist,* where the other (*to heteron*) is indeed simply opposed to the one, but he quickly adds another example, which strikes much closer to home for readers even moderately familiar with Hegel's own system. The example is the relationship of spirit to nature (ibid.). When we conceive nature's difference from spirit as nature's *absolute* otherness in relation to spirit we are, in effect, setting up two independent entities, where we ought to be thinking of nature as the embodiment and the expression of the life of spirit (such is, as we know, the approach of that *Naturphilosophie* that Hegel himself, following Schelling, considered to be the correct interpretive stance towards natural phenomena). To be sure, this example has its obvious drawbacks in that it employs conceptions (especially the conception of nature) which are not stages in the strictly logical unfolding of Logos. Nature is, for Hegel, the logical Idea externalized and dispersed in space and time. But, on the other hand, Hegel can legitimately consider nature only qua conception—and this conception is now (in the example given) a distorted one, since nature should by no means be thought of as absolutely different from spirit. Hegel makes this important point rather casually ("However, since spirit is . . . " etc.; ibid.), as if taking for granted our familiarity with his philosophy of nature; but we must remember that the example is simply used as an outside help to (and not a justification of) a purely conceptual argument that follows immediately after the example. We recall what has happened when we tried to assert, at an earlier stage, the independence of the quality from its bearer: we were soon forced to reunite these two moments *within* the quality itself. We are now being taught the same lesson at a higher and more sophisticated stage of thinking: "The other simply by itself is the other *in its own self*, hence the other *of itself* . . . " (*SL* 118; my emphasis). We began by manufacturing an additional something: we separated what determines from what is determined (the "what" from the "that" we may say, as long as we keep in mind that both the "what" and the "that" are still too abstract to be thought of as essence and existence) and we set up the moment of determinateness as an independent entity having a life of its own. But since that determinateness is now itself a something, it too *is*. It is both a "what" and a "that" and we find ourselves—once again—confronted with the task of thinking the unity of these two moments. We *may*, of course, stubbornly persist in manufacturing still another something out of the determinateness of the something we have already manufactured; but this will not save us from our predicament, as we will quickly rediscover within the new something the very same two moments (a determinateness and a bearer determined by it) which we were trying to separate. Since these two items are thus inseparable under any description we may want to give them, there is no escape from the obligation of thinking them together.

Hence the next stage of the dialectic of "Something and Other." The other (the determinateness) is now clearly recognized as the other *of* its something. But as we are still unable to give an account of their unity, we are forced to see them drift apart once more: "The otherness is at once contained in it [in something] and also still *separate* from it; it is a *being-for-other*" (*SL* 119). The content of what is now under consideration includes both moments: the bearer and its determinateness, the determinateness and its bearer. But this content can be considered in two different forms, which have no connection with each other. Insofar as this content is considered independently of any relations to external observers, it is a mere being-in-itself, a mere existent, void of any identifiable qualities. Insofar, however, as this content is considered as standing in some such relations to observers, it is viewed as endowed (in, and due to, the eye of the beholder, to be sure) with a wealth of determinations. We don't have to engage in a guessing game in order to discover Hegel's target in this analysis. The target is the Kantian notion of *Ding-an-sich* (*SL* 120) and its contradictions. For Kant, any property that we attribute to reality is dependent upon our mode of cognition. This is what Kant infers not only as the consequence of his transcendental arguments meant to justify our synthetic a priori knowledge of nature, but also as the only way to escape the pitfalls of the antinomies. We have no knowledge, Kant concludes, of reality as it is, or may be, in itself, i.e., independently of our cognitive perspective. At the same time, however, Kant is forced to talk about reality as it is "in itself" (i.e., independently of how it appears to human knowers). For Kant considers it to be both the source of the affections of our sensibility (*CPR*, B522, A494) and a limiting concept (of "noumenon" in the negative sense) which we must employ in order to restrict the soaring ambition of our knowledge (*CPR*, B310–11).

In all of his major works Hegel advances against Kant an argument that is here (*SL* 121) compressed in a few lines and reduced to its bare bones so as to give us a clear and firm grasp of the basic conceptual shortcoming of Kantian criticism. Its present failure is the very opposite of what went wrong earlier, due to our hasty imputation of independence to the determinateness, to the "what" of a something. We are now trying to think a "that" without assigning any "what" to it. We thus end up with an empty abstraction, for we want to talk about an entity without attributing to it an identity; or rather, the only identity we are prepared to attribute to the thing-in-itself is sheer *being* (for the thing-in-itself, in Kant, does not owe its existence to our cognitive apparatus). But this is highly unilluminating and it does not even allow us to decide whether we ought to talk about (one) "thing-in-itself" or (many) "things-in-themselves"—both terms appear, side by side, in Hegel's present argument, his intention being, most likely, to stress the ambiguity of Kant's position—since we are not warranted to employ the category of quantity.

We are thus led to abandon the (formal) distinction of "in itself" and "for other." We must abolish it not only in content—as we already did at the beginning of the present move—but in form as well. The something ought not to be construed as identical with—and identifiable by—its determinateness only insofar as we consider the something in relation to an observer, or to what is in general outside of the something. The "that" of an entity must entertain a necessary, internal relation with its "what." The presence of its determinateness is constitutive to (and of) an entity. When we succeed, at first very imperfectly, in thinking the internal relation between the two moments of the something—between its that and its what—the determinateness of the something becomes the something's determination (*Bestimmung*) (*SL* 122).

The rendering of *Bestimmung* through "determination" does not, however, do full justice to the German meaning of the word. *Bestimmung* is not mere determination, but determination viewed as "destiny" or "calling" or "vocation." That this is indeed what Hegel has in mind becomes clear from the example given at the very beginning of the present section ("Determination, Constitution and Limit"). "The determination of man," says Hegel, "is thinking reason" (*SL* 123)—and reason is here not a mere fact of human nature but a task, a norm for man to take up and to act upon by exhibiting a truly rational behavior and thought. Let us shift back to the strictly logical category now being analyzed: the category of "something." Determination, then, is the something's determinateness taken up and, we may say, internalized by the something itself. As we already saw, it is not possible to account for the something's qualities only in terms of its relations with what lies outside it—preferably in terms of its reference to an external human observer. For insofar as the something must have an identity and insofar as that identity is made up by the something's determinateness, the latter must belong to the very inner core of the something. And when we thus think of the something's determinateness as belonging to its inner core—to the something's "in itself" (*An sich*—*SL* 122)—the determinateness in question becomes the determination of the something. The identity we so foolishly derived from an external observer's presence now becomes the something's *own* identity—its own vocation, its calling. Thus every something is now endowed with a task—the task of fulfilling its own vocation. We can think here of the philosophy of Aristotle, where everything has an inner drive, a *hormē* to fulfill itself. The something is precisely such a striving to fulfill itself. "Determination implies that what something is *in itself*, is also *present in* it" (*SL* 123).

In determination, then, the something's identity is a vocation "present" to the something itself and the latter actively strives to fulfill the former. It is this new aspect of determination (as "present" to the something) that allows us to appreciate the progress accomplished in comparison to earlier, and less adequate, conceptions of determinateness. "Determination is affirmative determinateness as the in-itself with which something in its determinate being remains congruous in face of its entanglement with the other by which it might be determined, maintaining itself in its self-equality, and making its determination hold good in its being-for-other" (*SL* 123). The task of realizing or fulfilling its vocation means that the something must remain "faithful" to it throughout all the trials of its entire life history. All situations and challenges must be dealt with in conformity with the requirements of the something's determination. Let us return to Hegel's opening example. On the one hand, rational thinking may be seen—not at all incorrectly although still one-sidedly—as a mere determinateness, i.e., as a ready-made quality which distinguishes man from the brute. But this is not yet adequate to express what we mean when we say that man is a rational creature, since "thought is also present *in* him" (*SL* 123). Rationality is not simply a quality of man as man; it is also a self-imposed imperative to act and to think rationally, it is a task to be confronted and carried out. And, obviously, some men will fail in carrying out that task. Taken in this second sense, rationality cannot be viewed as a mere given, since it must first be won by the individual's own activity.

Now as long as the identity of the something is its vocation— i.e., only a vocation—the something *is not* (not yet, in any case) what it is meant to be. Furthermore, we cannot conceive this discrepancy between the something's being and the something's calling without introducing the concept of "constitution" (*Beschaffenheit*). The constitution is the element of inertia and passivity within the something, the element which does not allow the something to exist in (full) conformity with its calling. For example, "in contrast" (*SL* 123) to man's rationality we must posit his anchorage in nature in general, i.e., his status as a creature subject to his own blind impulses as well as to the blind forces of his external environment. Due to this constitution, man's rationality is hampered by influences which are inimical to it.

Determination and constitution are thus posited, at first, as merely external to each other. As hampering the fulfillment of the something's vocation, the constitution "does not belong to the something's in-itself" (*SL* 124). We soon come to see, however, that determination and constitution must be construed as standing in a more intimate relationship. For the vocation of an entity is to be realized not only in spite of, but also within that entity's constitution. Thus, in man, the task of being rational calls for a successful imposition of a rational discipline upon that crude nature inside and outside him. Since man cannot escape from his anchorage in nature, the imperative to be rational can require nothing more than the transformation of nature in conformity with the principles of reason. Let us not forget, however, that man's rational vocation is here only an example with the aid of which Hegel hammers away at a conceptual necessity. In general, then, we cannot ignore the gap between the something's determination and its constitution; *but* we must also take into account their internal relation. Thus we were mistaken in supposing that the determinateness of the something is to be construed as (only) the something's determination. The constitution of the something is just as essential to the something's identity—to its "in-itself"—as is its vocation. A more complete conception of the something's determinateness is now required, a conception which would encompass both the determination (the vocation) *and* the constitution of the something (*SL* 124).

The next stage, then, is as follows. The something's striving to fulfill its vocation takes place within its given constitution, but the constitution itself is formed and shaped by that striving. The original, merely given, constitution is thus altered by the something's striving to fulfill its vocation. "This alteration of something is no longer the alteration of something merely in accordance with its being-for-other [. . .] now alteration is also *posited* in the something" (*SL* 125). The something's alteration, that is, is self-induced and self-generated: it is due to the something's own striving to fulfill its vocation by actively changing its own constitution.

The fulfillment of a something's vocation is, however, its undoing. For example, a flourishing civilization lives up to its potential, fulfills its (historical) task and then leaves the scene of history; another civilization will then take its place, being both the result and the cancellation of the first civilization's development. Similarly, the fulfillment of a seed's determination amounts to the disappearance of the seed itself and to the birth of the plant. We end up with "*two* somethings" (*SL* 125) which entertain an entirely new and complex relation with each other. Insofar as the plant is the fulfillment of the seed's own vocation, it is not indifferent to and unconnected with the seed itself—the plant is the term of the seed's own development. But the plant is also a different entity, with a vocation of its own. In the plant the seed both externalizes itself and perishes as a seed. A new notion—the notion of the something's passing over into (*SL* 125) or "ceasing . . . in" (*SL* 126) an other something—is called for to articulate this newly reached stage of the dialectic Finitude: "the other is only externally opposed to the *first* something, or rather, since in fact they are *directly* connected, that is in their Notion, their connection is this, that determinate being has *passed over* into otherness, something into other, and something is just as much an other as the other itself is" (*SL* 125).

We have just witnessed the emergence of a new category—of limit (*Grenze*)—and the development of this category will allow us to gain a better grasp of the inherent finitude of every something. Let us first be clear as to what we now mean when we say that a thing has a "limit." Since we have not yet arrived at any conception of Quantity, the limit we have in mind is only a qualitative one (*Enc.* I, #92). When we talk about limit in this sense we intend to signal that the something has a concrete, specific identity, i.e., that the something cannot lose certain kinds of features or accommodate certain kinds of changes without, in effect, ceasing to be itself. We remember, too, that we have passed the stage where a bearer and its identity were merely superimposed upon each other by an external reflection. The *Grenze* as the identity of a something is the fulfilled vocation of that something; and every something must be viewed as striving to reach its own limit by fulfilling its vocation. But—and this is the second feature of the something's limit—in fulfilling its vocation the something both accomplishes itself and exhausts itself in another something (a seed in a plant, etc.) and it then goes under. The something's destruction is thus brought about by the something's own self-realization. In striving to fulfill itself the something prepares the ground for its own undoing; the possession of a limit in the sense of a specific identity means also the possession of a limited career as a distinct entity.

The detailed dialectic of limit moves through several stages. Limit is, first, that in which and due to which an entity asserts its distinctness from other entities: "Something [. . .] has a limit, in the first place, relatively to an other; the limit is the non-being of the other" (*SL* 126). Thus the seed is *not* the plant, the plant is *not* the seed, etc. We cannot posit anything as a distinct entity without distinguishing it from other entities; as we recall, for Hegel too *omnis determinatio est negatio*. Furthermore, the distinctness of an entity is not secured by the negation of just *any* other entity. The negation is not indifferent to its terms—and this is why the negation is informative, this is why it tells us something nontrivial about the entity in question—but it represents a contrast within a system or within a domain to which these terms belong. For example, a plant is distinguished from a seed, but not, say, from the number 3. Thus, in Hegel's own examples, the moon is distinguished from the sun (*Enc.* I, #92), a line from a point (*SL* 127), etc.

But limit is not only the something's "non-being of the other." Equally, if not more importantly, limit is what allows the something's actual, present form to be continuous with its future forms; due to a something's limit all stages of its development are seen as expressions of that something's concrete identity, of its enduring quality as this or that: *"through the limit something is what it is, and in the limit it has its quality"* (SL 126).

Let us put together these two aspects of limit. According to the first aspect, the something's limit means that the something *is not* (for it is distinct from another something). According to the second aspect, the something's limit means that the something *is* (for it has a positive, enduring identity). Our first clumsy attempt to conceive these two aspects of limit takes the path of immediacy, and thus the two aspects are held apart: "Now insofar as something in its limit both *is* and is *not* and these moments are an immediate, qualitative difference, the negative determinate being and the determinate being of the something fall outside each other" (*SL* 127). We end up with two entities which "have their determinate being *beyond* each other" (ibid.). In other words, we first consider the thing in its inner identity (the limit in the sense of what the thing *is*) and only then—as an additional step—do we also consider the thing in its distinctness from other things (the limit in the sense of what the thing *is not*).

Naturally, given what we already know about *Grenze*, we can anticipate that the separation of the "is" and the "is not" moments of limit will not be able to sustain itself. A seed "is" its limit (the seed's specific, concrete identity) only insofar as it fulfills itself in its other, i.e., in what the seed "is not" (in the plant): "the something which *is* only in its limit [the first moment of limit], just as much separates itself from itself and points beyond itself to its non-being [the second moment of limit], declaring this to be its being and thus passing over into it" (*SL* 127–28). Thus the seed fulfills its identity (what the seed is) by giving birth to the plant (the *non*-being of the seed) or, again, a point fulfills itself in becoming a line.[12] In general (*SL* 128) every something is full of "unrest" (*Unruhe des Etwas*) to become another something. We have returned to an earlier station in our journey through the land of *Etwas*, except that now the "other" something (the plant) is posited within the original something (the seed): what the something "is not" is now immanent (*SL* 129) to what it "is." Due to the something's very finitude (due to the something's having a determinate identity as its own limit, as what the something is) the something will alter (and thus become another something, something it is not). An *Etwas*, Hegel sums up, "is by its very quality firstly *finite*, secondly *alterable*; so that finitude and variability appertain to its being" (*Enc.* I, #92).

The disappearance of a something is, for now at least, a mere disappearing: when the something lives out its limit, it abandons the stage to another something. This is why the first paragraph of the concluding subsection on finitude is entitled "The Immediacy of Finitude." In this paragraph the something's disappearance is brought out only in its (immediately given and observable) negative moment: the something was, and now it is not. Its entire destiny was to perish. This is the aspect that our thought now seizes upon and isolates: "finitude is the negation as *fixed in itself*, and it therefore stands in abrupt contrast to its affirmative" (*SL* 130). These expressions return here again and again under Hegel's pen. The "affirmative" aspect of the finite—the aspect which is being glossed over but will soon come to the fore—is nothing other than the preservation of the finite in (and in spite of) its very destruction. Finite beings go under and pass away but, we shall soon learn, they are also saved from lapsing into total nonbeing insofar as they are moments of the infinity; for they return to infinity—albeit in a changed form—even while undergoing the process of destruction. As Hegel puts it in his *Philosophy of Religion*,[13] at the present, still merely immediate, stage of finitude, our thinking is attentive only to the "justice" of infinity (i.e., only to the death sentence passed upon each and every finite being), but not to its "goodness" (to the finite entities' preservation from nonbeing and oblivion by the saving power of infinity). Of course we are not yet attending to the category of infinity itself. But, at the same time, the two aspects of the finite—the negative-destructive aspect and the affirmative-preserving aspect—are due to the finite beings' standing within the infinite.

Moreover, this presence of the infinite as the background which allows the finite to appear even in its first (negative-destructive) moment imposes itself quickly in spite of our exclusive focus upon the finite. For what happens when we are attending carefully to the "transitoriness" of finite beings? This very transitoriness becomes what is "imperishable" and "abso-

lute"; transitoriness itself "is thus eternal" (*SL* 130). The truth
that all things must pass away is itself an unchangeable truth;
and as the Hegelian Logos unfolds, from the very beginning, on
a level where the separation of truth and being is no longer
operative, being itself emerges here as an unchangeable. This is
the first form in which we witness the emergence of something
that extracts itself from disappearing and passing away. And
since every finite being—i.e., every limited being—must disappear and pass away, the eternal is at first posited as the polar
opposite of the finite. We thus discover and move on to the first
stage of infinity.

Given what we have already argued earlier, in our analysis of
the "great triad" of Being-Nothing-Becoming, it will come as
no surprise to us that Hegel talks here repeatedly (*SL* 129, 130)
about the "sadness" (*Trauer*) with which thinking apprehends
the merely negative status of the finite. The presence of *human
moods and sentiments,* we have argued, is not accidental but
indeed constitutive to the intelligibility of the process of pure
thinking. Thus, the positing of pure being, as well as its passing
over into pure nothing and, finally, their coalescence into becoming turned out to be intelligible only to a thinker lucidly
aware of his own mortality; and such awareness, we remember,
was conditioned by the presence of a *Gesinnung* of "indifference." This very special mood or sentiment supplied the
context and the background within which the great triad was
laid out by, and for, pure thought. Hegel's present references to
the "sadness" of the thought of (mere) disappearing—i.e., of
the *irrevocability of death*—are a further testimony that an ever
present sense of the *human condition* underlies the stages and the
stations of the unfolding Logos.

As we pointed out a moment ago, we catch the first glimpse
of infinity even while thinking through to its very end the irre-
vocable transitoriness of all finite beings. Thus, in contemplat-
ing the disappearing of everything that is finite we set up a realm
of reality which is not threatened by transitoriness. These two
realms are now sharply opposed and split apart: the finite is *not*
the infinite, the infinite is *not* the finite. But to posit our two
realms in this way is to set the stage for a most severe contradiction. For in this way the finite remains something standing on
its own account—"it remains absolute on its own side" (*SL*

130)—and thus the infinite is not truly infinite since it does not encompass the realm of the finite. By being independent of the infinite, the finite limits the infinite. To be truly infinite, the infinite must succeed—and must be thought of as succeeding—in absorbing the finite. For the sake of the infinite's very infinity, the finite *ought* not to be independent of the infinite.

With this last new term—the ought, *Das Sollen*—the next stage of the dialectic of finitude is reached: Limitation and the Ought. This is, we are told (*SL* 136, *Enc.* I, #94), the Kant-Fichte standpoint; but the forthcoming analyses and the refutations apply above all to Fichte and only marginally to Kant. For the concept of "limitation" (*Schranke*)—in contrast to the earlier concept of mere "limit" (*Grenze*)—is nothing other, we shall soon see, than the Fichtean ego's *self*-limitation in the process of (and as an opportunity for) asserting the ego's own infinity. And no such idea appears in Kant even if Fichte claimed—against Kant's protestations, to be sure—that he was simply systematizing the corpus of critical philosophy.

When the something was still thought as endowed with a mere limit, its determination (its vocation, its destiny) was to fulfill itself and then to (simply) die. When limit becomes limitation, the finite is to be brought under the power of the infinite. The finite is now set up as *not* independent of the infinite; and the proper action of the infinite will now consist in *demonstrating* its power over the finite. And this demonstration is precisely the striving of the Fichtean ego, aiming to vanquish the resistence of limitations posited by the ego itself. Hegel's present criticism of Fichte compresses the results of his earlier polemics, going back as far as Hegel's early essay *Glauben and Wissen*.

Let us turn, then, to the subsection of *Science of Logic* titled "Limitation and the Ought." As against the preceding stage identified as "The Immediacy of Finitude," two crucial and interdependent shifts have taken place. First, the limit has become the limitation; second, the infinite has become the ought.

To begin with the first shift, the something now sets up its own limit, which thus becomes the something's *self*-imposed limitation (*SL* 132). Thus, we noted, Fichte's infinite ego limited itself. But the infinite ego, while thus limited itself, still remains infinite; in fact, the ego's self-limitation is due to its own impulse to demonstrate its very infinity through a successful

overcoming of what is not infinite. Without such a demonstration the ego's initial claim to be infinite would have been but an
empty pretension to begin with. Thus—and this is the second
shift now taking place—the limitation is set up only as something that ought not to be; conversely, what ought to be is the
infinite ego insofar as it confirms its domination over the limitation. Just as limit, then, passed over into limitation, infinity
passed over into a task, into what ought to be. The two new
moments are interconnected: we cannot have limitation without the ought, and we cannot have the ought without limitation
(*SL* 133). If the ego were not limited in some way, it would not
have to *strive* to be infinite—its infinity would then be a given
and not a task disclosed in an ought. But if the ego actually
strives to become infinite by imposing itself upon what limits it
(its environment, its own inclinations, etc.), then this can only
be, Fichte argued and Hegel concurs, if what limits the ego is
thought of as malleable by the ego's power; and this, in turn, is
intelligible only if the ego's limits are not imposed upon it (as
they still were in Kant) by something foreign to it, but only by
the ego itself.

This new, Fichtean, stage in the chapter on "Determinate
Being" is reflected in the terminology Hegel now employs: "in
this relation the determination [*Bestimmung*] is an ought [*Sollen*]" (*SL* 132). The implicit reference to Fichte's semipopular
treatise *The Vocation of Man* (*Die Bestimmung des Menschen*) is
unmistakable: it is the vocation of man, Fichte held, to live up to
the moral *Sollen*. In thus living up to his highest calling a human
agent overcomes and vanquishes the inertia and the resistance of
his lower, limited self and he thus transcends himself: "since the
limit is in the *determination* itself as a limitation, something
transcends *its own self*" (*SL* 132).

It can be objected at once that Hegel's analysis of *Schranke*
and *Sollen* is meant to apply to the general category of something (*Etwas*) and not exclusively to the (more restricted)
category of human self. But Hegel's position on this particular
issue is highly ambiguous. On the one hand, we are told that the
(recently deduced) notion of self-transcending is meaningless
when applied to "stone" and "metal"; for, Hegel points out (*SL*
134), the limitations of such unthinking and unfeeling entities
do not exist for those entities. This is why we are not even

warranted in talking about a stone's limitation, but only about its "limitedness" (*Beschranktheit*—*SL* 134). On the other hand, however, "even the stone *as a something*, contains the distinction and it too transcends . . . its limitation" (ibid.; my emphasis). How, then, does a stone differ from a plant or an animal, not to mention a human self? The difference seems to be that a sentient creature has an inner "urge to overcome this limitation [of hunger, thirst, etc.]" and that such a creature overcomes its limitation "in its own strength" (*SL* 135); while the inorganic matter, Hegel explains, changes only due to an *external* impact: thus, in Hegel's example, a base being acted upon by an acid. Nevertheless, insofar as they have at least a disposition to undergo change when brought together, "the ought, the obligation to transcend limitations, is present in both acid and caustic base" (*SL* 135).

It is not my intention to minimize these ambiguities (not to say outright contradictions!), but I think we can circumvent them, at least within the context of Hegel's present interests. For whether the ought and the limitation are or are not embodied (and if so, where and to what extent) outside of the area of human agency, it is clear that what matters to Hegel is the discrepancy, the gap between *Sein* and *Sollen*. And no such gap can be found even in the area of organic nature: "the individual plant does not become untrue to its nature; it becomes what it ought to be; in it Being and destined character are not different. This separation in anything between what ought-to-be, and its nature, first makes its appearance with free-will."[14]

Due to this separation of *Sein* and *Sollen,* the contradiction between the finite and the infinite will now reemerge within the self, for "the ought is the transcending, but still only *finite transcending,* of the limitation" (*SL* 135).

The expression "finite transcending" (*endliches Hinausgehen*) both pins down the contradiction inherent in the present category and sets the stage for our thought's first move to resolve the contradiction. The transcending is (1) the *transcending* of the finite; and, to that extent, it is an unceasing effort to escape the bonds of finitude. But the transcending is also (2) the transcending *of the finite* (and not of something else) and, to that extent, it cannot liberate itself from the weight of the finite. This connection between the finite and its transcending is, moreover, necessary. The finite supplies the stimulus and is the adversary for the action of transcending: if it were not for the presence of the finite, there would be no need for an action to abolish the finite's independence. Thus transcending feeds upon the very adversary that it aims at annihilating. And this is, in effect, the very main contradiction of the (presently conceptualized) "moral view of the world"[15]—man must strive to achieve the aim of subjecting his inclinations to the moral law, and yet the achievement of this aim would eliminate moral striving as such. As long, then, as we are committed to the categories of ought and limitation, we must rule out the possibility of the moral striving's ever reaching its satisfaction.

The stage is now set for the transition from finitude as a whole to infinity. With the conception of moral striving the thought of finitude received its most sophisticated expression. The Fichtean ego is the conjunction of the limitation and the ought, where the limitation is already posited by the ego itself. Still, even though they both spring from the same source— from the ego—the ought and the limitation are held apart, they are "qualitatively opposed" (*SL* 136). This is the first thing Hegel wants us to keep in mind when leading us up to transition from finitude to infinity. Second, this qualitative opposition is not a state of peaceful coexistence between *Sein* and *Sollen*. The limitation is posited as adverse to the ought—as something to be overcome by the striving of the *Etwas*. But the something that so strives is a finite something and hence what will appear as the product of striving will be burdened by finitude: "in ceasing to be, the finite has not ceased to be; it has become in the first instance only *another* finite which, however, is equally a ceasing-to-be as transition into another finite, and so on to *infinity*" (*SL* 136). As soon as the moral self succeeds in vanquishing this or that inclination, another inclination must emerge—if it did not, the agent would cease to be finite—and the struggle will be repeated again and again.

The exercise of this striving, however, brings us to the threshold of a new category: of infinity. "Closer consideration of this result shows that the finite in its ceasing-to-be, in this negation of itself has attained its being-in-itself, is *united with itself*. [. . .] This *identity with itself*, the negation of negation is affirmative being and the other of the finite [. . .] this other is the *infinite*"

(*SL* 136–37). The moral striving is an infinite task, since it can never be fulfilled in any actual performance of the agent—it aims at a goal which is forever beyond the agent's reach. But this task is taken seriously and acted upon by the agent himself in a kind of "hope against hope" attitude which, to be sure, can bear no practical fruits—for the goal is always beyond the agent's grasp—but which nevertheless makes the agent aware of his own dignity and heroism. In taking up and in responding to the infinite task of *Sollen* the agent has, in a way, given testimony to his own infinity. Every failed—inevitably failed—attempt to live up to the infinite task makes the agent aware that the home of infinity is within him.

When so defined, infinity becomes the affirmative determination of the something. While still remaining a vocation, a calling of finite beings, this infinity not only cancels the finite but also lifts it up and preserves it within the realm of the infinite. To return to the language of *Philosophy of Religion:* the infinity of the ought was all "justice" but no "goodness"; the ought's function was to deny and to destroy the limitation. The rule of that merely negative form of infinity was: let the finitude *not* be. The rule is now: let the finitude (truly) *be* through a merger with the infinite. While this second rule still demands the negation of finitude, it does not demand the *mere* negation any more, for it gives the finite a positive and higher identity: the finite is to be lost as finite only to recover itself as being in and of the infinite.

We have now abandoned altogether the area of finitude. For if the infinite is the true nature of the something—of every finite something—then the only destiny still left to the finite is to merge with the infinite. The finite, that is, must be stripped of any autonomy and self-subsistence; and the finite must undergo this process not as a result of an alien power, but through its own efforts to live up to its newly discovered vocation. The finite thus sublates itself in the infinite "and what *is*, is only the *infinite*" (*SL* 138). From the dualism of Fichte we have moved to the modern, Schellingian version of Eleatic philosophy of the absolute as the infinite and undifferentiated one. We are thus (1) brought back to the great triad, but (2) the great triad itself has acquired a more specific form due to the road behind us. Let us consider these two points separately.

The very opening sentence of the section on infinity gives the

familiar names to the land we have just discovered: "The infinite
in its simple Notion can, in the first place, be regarded as a fresh
definition of the absolute; as indeterminate self-relation it is
posited as *being* and *becoming*" (*SL* 137). Clearly, (1) in some
sense we are back at the logical beginning of thought at the stage
of indeterminate, pure being which cannot be posited without
becoming nothing. The very abstractness of these notions was
meant to guarantee their unconditioned, absolute character. To
start with a more specific category would have meant taking
something for granted ("presupposing" something), and such
an attitude would have been incompatible with the fundamental
impulse of philosophical speculation. Hegel's reason for ascribing kinship with pure being to the present conception of infinity
becomes clear now. We have learned that every determination is
a negation, that every determinate being must have a limit.
Since—as we have learned further—every limited being is
finite, no determinate being can be infinite; only the pure, undifferentiated being, it now seems to us, can be infinite. But (2)
all of this also represents some progress over the notion of pure
being from the great triad. The notion of infinity is more specific
than the original pure being, at least insofar as this notion is
enriched through its contrast with our (by now fairly specified
and articulate) conception of the finite. No such conception of
the finite was available to us at the beginning of *Logic,* and thus
the self-enclosedness of pure being could have been compatible
with some form of "a limitedness of which being and becoming
could have been capable" (*SL* 137). This has now been ruled out
and we have learned that pure being must be thought of as
infinite. What was then still lacking to give the Parmenidean
sphere this further and more specific determination was, of
course, the modern Christian notion of a finite self engaging in
the struggle to extirpate and uproot its own finitude, opting
finally, with Schelling and with the Romantics, to merge with
the infinite, whose sublimity and elevation are such that at its
very "name . . . the heart and the mind light up" (*SL* 138).

　　We have not, so far, progressed beyond the first subsection of
the infinity part of the chapter on determinate being. With the
next subsection—titled "Alternating Determination of the
Finite and the Infinite"—we discover the contradiction of infinity. In effect, just as we have seen the finite abolish itself in the

infinite, so too we will see the infinite becoming a spurious infinity and thus abolishing itself as infinite.

The contradiction of the present stage can be outlined in the following terms. At the beginning of the part on infinity we have succeeded in redefining pure being as infinity. Doubtlessly, this did represent some progress over the abstractness of the great triad. The pure being itself has received a more specific form of determinateness. However, precisely in its status of a determinate conception, the infinite can only be grasped through a contrast with its opposite: the finite. The infinite is *not* the finite; the infinite asserts itself as what it is only by distinguishing itself from the finite. Thus the finite lies beyond the boundaries of the infinite; the finite is *not* the infinite—and so the finite, in turn, asserts itself as what it is by distinguishing itself from the infinite. Hence our conception of infinity "resuscitates the *being* of its negation, of the finite again" (*SL* 138–39).

A more precise clarification of this rebirth of the finite can now be supplied. The infinite, we remember, was meant to be the affirmative, not the negative, infinity. This the infinite now is, but so far only as "simply affirmative" (*SL* 134). On the one hand, the ought is behind us, for the finite has accomplished the feat of actually merging with the infinite. On the other hand, however, the price of this exploit has been exorbitant, for the finite has abdicated any standing of its own vis-à-vis the infinite. The very success of the merger—the "simply affirmative" total absorption of the finite by the infinite—is thus setting the stage for its own undoing. For as determinate—as infinite and not finite—the infinite demands to be put in contrast with the finite. The finite (the finite as *opposed* to the infinite) is thus reborn as a result of our very attempt to dissolve it in the infinite.

This rebirth of the finite, moreover, brings under suspicion the kind of determinateness we have so recently and so proudly ascribed to the infinite. The infinite is indeed determinate insofar as it is qualified—as the original pure being was not—by its contrast with the finite. But in this pair it is the finite which is a *"real determinate being"* (*SL* 138) (only the finite has colors, or odors, or feelings and desires, etc.). The infinite's whole determinateness consists only in *not* being the finite; the infinite is thus, in point of fact, "the indeterminate void" (*SL* 139). We

cannot lay our hands on the determinateness of the infinite, for
every concrete determinateness belongs to the finite and, therefore, cannot be attributed to the infinite. The infinite is always
beyond each and every concrete determination; it is merely the
ever-eluding "beyond of the finite" (ibid.). Since such infinite is
not—as the infinite was meant to be—*in* the finite, but *outside*
the finite, we are confronted immediately with two distinct
realms set apart from each other. And yet—this is the root of the
contradiction we will now face—we cannot think these two
realms as independent of each other. Not only does the finite
find its calling in the merger with the infinite, but the latter
cannot establish itself *as* infinite otherwise than through its contrast with the finite; and thus the presence of the finite is implied
by the infinite just as strongly as the presence of the infinite is
implied by the finite: "each is in its own self and through its own
determination the positing of its other, they are *inseparable*. But
this their unity is *concealed* in their *qualitative* otherness" (*SL*
141). Since the unity of the finite and the infinite is thus "concealed"—i.e., not thought out—it will emerge as a brute,
incomprehensible given each time we attempt to think either of
them. We think the infinite and then "the finite appears as a
happening external to the infinite . . . "; the finite is thus
"found as given" (ibid.) by a way of thinking surprised by the
results of its own mode of operation. But as soon as we set our
gaze upon this finite we are thrown back upon the infinite (with
which the finite must merge). Our thought agitates itself in a
never-ending slide from the finite to the infinite and from the
infinite to the finite. The "simply affirmative" infinity can now
be given a new and very famous label: it is a *spurious infinity*
(*schlechte Unendlichkeit*—*SL* 142), for our attempt to think it
can never come to completion. Within the sphere of infinity we
have rediscovered "the perennial ought" (ibid.).

Let us quickly point out that this discovery is not a throwback to the (earlier) stage of Limitation and Ought. For the
reemergence of the ought is due, this time, to the reassertion of
the rights of the finite; and thus the ought itself presents us now
with an entirely different challenge than it did before. The challenge is, in fact, the very opposite of the problem represented by
the ought in the part on finitude. We cannot solve the present
problem by simply erasing the finite through its merger with the

infinite. Rather, the temptation would be to take the opposite approach: since we have just seen that the finite is essential to our thought, we could be tempted to deny the infinite. But this too would be self-defeating since we have also seen the incompleteness of the finite when posited as self-subsistent (i.e., without the infinite).

In any case—and much more importantly for Hegel's present argument—such temptations do not even present themselves to a thinking dedicated to its own integrity. We have arrived at a stage where "One only needs to *be aware of what one is saying* in order to find the determination of the finite in the infinite" (*SL* 143). Language imposes its own requirements which must be reflected upon, since language is the incarnation of Logos itself.[16] Thus we have no choice but to attempt to think the required unity of the finite and the infinite.

The acknowledgment of this requirement is in itself a progress compared to our earlier encounter with spurious infinity. In that encounter, we recall, the finite and the infinite were merely *found* together—"alongside each other" would be a better description of their initial indifference—and that raw givenness of their coexistence was then "not reflected on" (*SL* 142). We have now become aware that the finite and the infinite are not only found together, but *belong* together. We have risen to the thought of there being an essential connection between them; neither of them, we now realize, can exist (or even be defined) independently of each other. At the same time this essential connection of the finite and the infinite is not yet thought out and made intelligible. Their connection, then, is at once essential and external (*SL* 144), and this is the reason why the main contradiction will soon appear again, albeit in a more complex and more sophisticated form. The contradiction must appear, for we cannot have it both ways—either it is the case that the connection between A and B is indeed essential, but then it must also be the case that that connection is not merely external and indifferent to each of the two terms; or, if the connection is external and indifferent, we cannot think of it as being essential to the terms under consideration.

What would be involved in a (self-defeating) attempt to think as merely external the admittedly essential connection between the finite and the infinite? The analyses that follow in response to this question are a striking corroboration of Hegel's general rule: we can never solve a contradiction merely by relocating it from the *content* to the *form* of a conception.

The conception now under consideration is the unity of the finite and the infinite. This unity we are now prepared to acknowledge, but only insofar as the content of these items is concerned. As we saw, the finite sublated itself in the infinite, while the infinite limited itself in and by the finite. Now we recognize that the finite and the infinite must, therefore, "lose their qualitative nature" (*SL* 144)—i.e., their qualitative difference—by sharing in each other's qualities. Thus the infinite becomes the "finitized infinite," while the finite becomes the "infinitized finite" (*SL* 145). But this mutual sharing of each other's qualities is accomplished only in content, not in form. When we consider the (by now essential) unity of the finite and the infinite in the form of inwardness, of what that unity is "in itself" (ibid.), then its aspect of infinity comes to the fore. When, instead, we change our point of view and consider that finite-infinite unity in the form of limit, of the "sheer other of the in-itself" (ibid.) then—and then only—the aspect of the finite stands out while the aspect of the infinite recedes into the background. To put it still differently, the finite and the infinite are now *one and the same entity,* but our reliance upon two different expressions—the "in itself" and (its) "sheer other"—reflects our inability to move beyond what is, in effect (in contemporary terms), a version of the double-aspect theory. For this reason the unity of the finite and the infinite remains a "double entity" (ibid.) and cannot sustain itself. The difference must be established not only in content but in form as well. If the infinite truly *is* the finite then the latter must belong just as strongly to the inner core (to the "in itself") of their unity as does the former. Conversely, too, the infinite cannot be absent from the (more superficial) formal perspective of the "sheer other of the in-itself." To be sure, a way will then have to be found for expressing our thought that the finite is also different from the infinite. But the price for articulating this difference cannot be the acceptance of the rigid language of the double-aspect theory. Already in the *Phenomenology of Spirit*[17] Hegel was poking fun at that theory, which acknowledges the unity of content only to split it again into two unrelated forms: *X* is *A* "insofar as" we take it in the form F, and the same X is B "insofar as" we take it in the form F^I. However, Hegel argues, since we cannot even describe X *via* F without also describing it *via* F^I, the formal separation is just as strained and impossible to sustain as was the separation in content.

On account of their difference in form, the infinite and the finite continue to be held apart in the "double unity" even while being thought as essential to each other. This is at the root of the present contradiction and this contradiction will soon destroy those very same formal distinctions we have appealed to in order to escape its grip. At the same time, something new—and more adequate as a tool for grasping the notions of the finite and the infinite—will emerge from these labors of thought. In contrast to what took place so far, we will soon see not only how the finite abolishes itself in the infinite (and vice versa), but also how the finite *finds* itself again in the infinite (and vice versa). We will thus be confronted with the finite and the infinite coming-to-be and ceasing-to-be in and from each other: we will be confronted with their *becoming* each other. And this will allow us to formulate the conception of true infinity (*wahrhafte Unendliche*).

We must reflect more carefully upon the present difficulty and upon how we got into it. We remember that the distinction between the two forms of the infinite-finite unity was made in response to the requirement of abolishing the infinite progression of spurious infinity. For even then the unity of the finite and the infinite forced itself upon us: when we thought the infinite we were driven to think the finite; conversely, our thought of the finite slid immediately into the thought of the infinite. Whenever we thought one moment, the other moment was popping up and confronting our thought as a brute, unintelligible givenness. The connection of the two moments was thus essential to them, but we were unable to *think* clearly their belonging together, and so we moved endlessly back and forth between the finite and the infinite. The interplay of those moments was, Hegel reminds us, "not yet posited as a *single unity*" (*SL* 147). But this also allows us now both to see the causes of our earlier failure and to clear the path towards the solution.

The infinite progression was "in the first place" (*SL* 146) (i.e., in spurious infinity) the merely *negative* relationship between the finite and the infinite. We posited the infinite; the infinite was then replaced by the finite, which was immediately replaced by the infinite, and so on. On this first model of the infinite progression "the transcending of each moment starts independently, as a *fresh* act" (*SL* 147; my emphasis). We have the first appearance of the infinite I^1 and then the new and unrelated appearances I^2, I^3, I^4, etc.; each of these appearances is separated from each other by the (equally discrete and unrelated to each other) appearances of the finite (F^1, F^2, F^3, F^4, etc.). It is precisely this model that we found ourselves forced to abandon—and justifiably so—in favor of our later distinction between the two forms of the finite-infinite unity. The collapse of that later distinction as well allows us to cast a more penetrating gaze at what is really happening in our thinking's endless slide from the finite to the infinite. For we have now come to recognize that these two moments cannot be set apart under any description—our last possible attempt to do so (through form, but not through content) has just abolished itself. The slide from the finite to the infinite can now cease to take the shape of spurious infinity. Let us begin by positing the finite. It is immediately sublated by the infinite, but—and this new state of affairs is due to the most recent developments—the finite is not simply negated and replaced by the infinite. Since the finite has recovered its identity with the infinite—even in form!—"in this process the finite is united only with itself, and the same is true of the infinite—so that the negation of the negation results in an *affirmation*" (*SL* 152; my emphasis). Thus the process does not have to start again—in a never-ending sequence of "fresh starts" of the finite—since the assertion of the infinite is now not at all exclusive of the finite. The finite is always already there, in the infinite, and so the infinite does not have to be pushed aside by a new emergence of the finite. Once again—but at a higher level—the completion of the "justice" of infinity by its "goodness" allows us to escape the compulsion to mindlessly destroy the finite only to see it reborn, stubbornly and endlessly, against our intention to exclude it.

The same results will be arrived at beginning with the infinite (*SL* 147). Let us start with the endless progression again. We posit the infinite and then the finite must and will appear again, thus replacing the infinite. Then the infinite will assert itself anew in a new "fresh start." We will have produced one infinite

I^1, at the beginning and then the disconnected appearances I^2, I^3, I^4, etc. But if the opening conception of the infinite is not exclusive of the finite, then the latter will not simply replace the former but will also preserve it; in passing over into the finite the infinite will not disappear, and thus we will not be confronted by a *new* infinite. There will only be one and the same infinite reflecting itself in and from the finite. While the endless repetition of spurious infinity can be represented in the image of a straight line, our present conception—of true infinity—calls forth the image of a circle (*SL* 149), where we move within one and the same finite-infinite unity.

Within its "true" conception, infinity is finally given the two functions it was always meant to have. For Hegel infinity is both: one of the moments in the finite-infinite pair *and* that pair as a (properly thought out) whole.[18] This whole as well as its two moments are now grasped "essentially only as a *becoming*, but [in contrast to becoming from the great triad] a becoming *further determined* in its moments" (*SL* 148).

Due to this last formulation we can rediscover the thread we have chosen to lead us through the labyrinth of the logical dialectic. The thinker's comprehension of his own mortality, we argued at the beginning, supplied the background within which the opening moves of the logical dialectic gained their intelligibility and truth. These moves represented the discovery and the exploration of becoming as the unity of being and nothing. To the extent, then, that the present stage of thinking reestablishes itself as a mode of thinking the becoming, this thinking too is carried out within the thinker's *existential attitude* of comprehending the finitude of his condition. Were the thinker to lose that sense and that acceptance of himself as mortal, he would not understand (much less assent to) the conception of true infinity. For in that conception, Hegel just told us, its two moments of the finite and of the infinite are grasped as radically unstable, as becoming each other; and the thinker's refusal to come to terms with his own radical vulnerability and insecurity in the world would have made him unable to confront such a conception. But precisely this conception remains—and will remain—the very framework of the dialectic.

We have also, by now, put more flesh upon that framework's mere bones. Becoming is now, in Hegel's phrase, *"further deter-*

mined," since our conception of it has been enriched by and filled with the conceptual harvest collected from our exploration of determinate being in all of its multifarious forms and shapes— from *determinate being as such,* through *Finitude* to *Infinity.*

III.   Being-for-Self

The conception of becoming not only concludes the chapter on Determinate Being but also allows Hegel to move on to and to define the meaning of the next category: Being-for-self. And this category, we remember from our motto, is for Hegel nothing less than "the fundamental notion of philosophy" (*Enc.* I, #95). Now since the emergence of being-for-self is due to the becoming of the finite and the infinite (*SL* 148) and since becoming as such can only be grasped given the thinker's comprehension of his own mortality, this comprehension is also necessary for the intelligibility and the truth of the category of Being-for-self.

A still further item must now be added to this dossier. Man's condition as a finite creature will now itself be made the topic of a philosophical articulation. For, I shall argue, the category of being-for-self is the conceptualization of man's understanding of his own self as he confronts his finitude and, due to that experience, asserts his identity as a specifically *human* self. Everything we will learn from Hegel's own analyses of being-for-self will, I submit, corroborate this interpretation.

Let us note, to begin with, that even the merely logical treatment of being-for-self is peppered with constant references to the human self, more specifically, to the human self-consciousness. These references supply the present background of Hegel's analyses. Self-consciousness, says Hegel, is "being-for-self as *consummated* and *posited*" (*SL* 158); and such a being-for-self cannot be met with in nature (*Enc.* I, #96). To be sure, Hegel's own *Naturphilosophie* does attempt to follow the emergence of being-for-self in the natural world. But such a philosophical understanding of nature is itself possible only given our prior grasp of the category of being-for-self and —I shall argue—this category qua logical is intelligible to us only to the extent that we understand our powerlessness in the face of death. Ultimately—and this too, I shall argue, can be extracted from Hegel's own analyses of being-for-self—this form of human self-understanding will lead us to the experience of violence as to its ground.

The logical transition from determinate being to being-for-self has already been made in the last stage of our treatment of infinity. True infinity just *is* the being-for-self as the unity of what has now become the "reality" and the "ideality" (*SL* 150). These two terms now replace, respectively, the "finite" and the "infinite"; and the change in terminology reflects the change in concepts. The change is due to the (already stressed) emergence of the becoming of the finite and of the infinite within the true infinity (which exists itself only as a becoming). In effect—we shall explain this transition in a moment—insofar as the finite and the infinite exist as a becoming within a whole (true infinity) which is itself in the process of becoming, the finite and the infinite acquire certain new features and these new features are captured in the vocabulary of "reality" and "ideality."

Hegel's opening salvo in his outline of the transition from infinity to being-for-self drives the point home: "Ideality can be called the *quality* of infinity but is essentially the process of *becoming*" (*SL* 150). The reason why Hegel deems it necessary to talk about "quality" becomes clear from the comments put forward at the beginning of the chapter on being-for-self (*SL* 157). The development of thought in the chapter on determinate being, Hegel reminds us, was due to the unacceptable tension between being and quality. A determinate being was thought of as something with both a "that" and a "what," i.e., as an entity with a determinateness. Our thinking was set in motion by the task to properly articulate the simultaneous unity and difference of being and determinateness. All throughout the sections on determinate being our thought could not achieve the required balance: determinateness was set apart from being; determinateness was always (for example as the vocation, or the ought, etc.) the negation of being. The last stage of this exclusive dialectic of being and quality was reached with the category of infinity, where the infinite was set up as the mere negation of the finite. The entire sphere of determinate being was thus the sphere of the unreconciled difference between

being and its own determinateness: the latter was a mere negation of the former (*SL* 157).

With the true infinity, however, the negation has itself been
negated. The finite (i.e., being) is not simply excluded and transcended by the infinite (as in the vocation, the ought, etc.), but
reconciled with it. This is the reason why we must substitute the
terms "reality" and "ideality" for those earlier terms "finite" and
"infinite": "With reference to reality and ideality, however, the
opposition of finite and infinite is grasped in such a manner that
the finite ranks as the real but the infinite as the 'ideal' . . ." (*SL*
150). Thus in being-for-self we are still dealing with a quality,
but with a quality which (as ideality) has run its full course by
returning into being: here "*qualitative* being finds its
consummation" (*SL* 157). An entity's determinateness, that is,
does not hover over and above that entity any more. The entity
(the "reality") is now fully permeated with its own determinateness (the "ideality"). For example—and we shall return to
this example again and again, for it provides the paradigm of
Hegel's analyses—the entire finite content of a human self (i.e.,
all of our desires, volitions, representations, etc.) becomes now
formed and shaped by the self's own activity. A *meaning* is
assigned to our desires, volitions, and representations; all of
them become organized by and expressive of the self's activity.
They are thus the "reality" in which the "ideality" of the self's
form-giving activity finds its embodiment.

The specific form of human selfhood that Hegel here has in
mind is the *self-consciousness*. A relatively extended description of
it is given right at the beginning (*SL* 158) of the chapter on
being-for-self—Hegel is thus giving us a fairly precise clue as to
what he will be concentrating on in the course of the chapter—
and this description remains fully in line with the treatment
accorded to self-consciousness in the appropriate parts of the
Phenomenology and of the *Encyclopaedia*.

Before focusing on self-consciousness, however, Hegel re-
views and recasts his definition of being-for-self in terms that he
thinks are closer to our ordinary language. This move—Hegel
undoubtedly goes farther than he should by calling it a "justification" (*SL* 155) of his philosophical notion of being-for-self—
is not out of step with the general strategy pursued in the *Science
of Logic,* since Hegel is convinced that the categories of Logos

are indeed embedded in our ordinary language and thought; thus a philosophical conception must, inevitably, have its roots in our ordinary ways of thinking and speaking. Now the explanation of ordinary discourse yields, at this point, the results convergent with the philosophical inquiry. The "being-for-self" as it has been deduced philosophically as the interplay of "ideality" and "reality" is the very same thing, Hegel thinks, that will be hit upon when we analyze the (ordinary) meaning of this idea. When we talk about a being which exists not only for another being, but also for itself, we implicitly put together the two philosophically relevant moments: there is, first, the moment of being, and then also, second, a clear indication that this being is here taken as existing for (its own) self. Or, again, the being is the "otherness" (*Das Anderssein*) of a self and this otherness exists *for* the self: "we say that something is for itself insofar as it transcends otherness, its connection and community with other, has repelled them and made abstraction from them. For it, the other has being only as sublated, as its *moment*" (*SL* 158). I am for myself, we may rephrase this point, insofar as I can collect myself from the merely given conditions of my life and thought. Instead of being a mere product of influences and entanglements foreign to me, I withdraw into myself in order to determine my own identity. The conditions of my life are, in this sense, only a "moment" to me, for what they mean and how they influence me will, from now on, depend upon myself. These conditions (the "otherness") are now taken up and absorbed within my own self, with all of its practical and cognitive powers. The moment of "otherness" is what we have already identified as the "reality" of being-for-self; while what that reality is absorbed within (i.e., the "ideality") is the self's own spiritual center.

With these preparatory remarks behind him, and given his particular angle of analysis, Hegel is ready to zero in on self-consciousness. Insofar as self-consciousness is self-*consciousness*, it has an internal reference to being, to reality; insofar as self-consciousness is *self*-consciousness, reality is subsumed under ideality. Let us take these two moments one by one. By "consciousness" (*Bewusstsein*) Hegel understands that particular level of our experience at which we objectify whatever it is that makes up the conditions of our life—our external environment, our body, our impulses and inclinations, and so on. All of this is gathered under the collective term "otherness." Consciousness, then, represents the level of experience in which this entire content of the self's life is displayed for the self as (still) independent of the self, as not yet formed by the self's powers. Hegel returns to this understanding of "consciousness" in many other places.[19] Taken merely as consciousness, the self is confronted with a brute givenness of reality. In contrast, the aspect of *self-consciousness* emerges precisely at the moment when the self begins to view reality as the embodiment of its own spiritual life. This absorption of reality by the self is, in fact, implied by the very notion of consciousness. For—and this is how Hegel pushes to its ultimate conclusions the idealism of Kant, who was *the* philosopher of the *Bewusstsein* standpoint (*Enc.* III, #415)— consciousness objectifies reality in a representation; but as the self cannot represent to itself anything that is not made by it, the self's ability to form a representation of reality proves that the latter is not alien and foreign to the self, but that it is (and must be seen as) an extension of the self. This does not mean that reality will now simply vanish. Self-consciousness remains self-*consciousness:* the moment of *Bewusstsein* is not wiped out but preserved, and hence the self continues to be aware of its environment, of its natural drives and inclinations and so on. But this entire content of the self's life is now re-made and re-formed by the self. Leibniz's monad, Hegel points out, (*SL* 161–63) is much closer to this notion of the self than anything to be found in the idealism of Kant or even of Fichte. For in Leibniz an individual's entire life history—with all of his cognitions, desires, and volitions—represents the unfolding of his own completely defined essence, while Kant, and even Fichte, left room for some impact of external conditions upon the self. This is why, Hegel continues to stress, both Kant and Fichte were unable to move beyond the standpoint of the ought, where the conditions of the self's existence are not yet fully absorbed within the self. Leibniz's system, much better on this point, goes, however, too far in the other direction: since all episodes in the life history of a monad flow from that monad's individual essence, the monad is entirely self-enclosed and hence its relations with an independent world remain unexplained (*SL* 162).

The self-enclosedness of the self is, nevertheless, the stage we are at right now. The first section of the chapter on being-for-self is titled "Being-for-self as such" and its three subsections hammer away at one and the same point: in its first emergence being-for-self asserts itself merely as an isolated, self-enclosed unit, as a "one." In the first subsection an explanation is offered as to why this is so. Being-for-self is a "one" for, as we already saw, being-for-self is *self*-determined. Being-for-self, that is, establishes and preserves its own identity throughout all the episodes of its career as an individual. All conditions of its existence are fully formed by the self's powers. The self is thus locked within its own enchanted world: whatever exists for the self bears the self's own stamp and represents an extension of the self. The self sees itself (and only itself) everywhere: what was formerly "the moment of determinate being is [now] present in being-for-self as a *being-for-one*" (*SL* 159).

This concluding sentence of the first subsection supplies the point of departure for a more detailed exploration of the being-for-one which will now follow (in the subsection titled "Being-for-one"). An entity's self-enclosedness must now be taken so literally and so extremely that we ought not even to allow ourselves the luxury of talking about *a* being-for-self. For in order to talk about *a* being-for-self we must consider it as a member of a community—a "one among many." But at the stage we are at right now there is nothing else *but* that unique self-enclosed self. From this abstract, solipsistic point of view, a community—actual or possible—can only be a moment in the unique self's representations. Hegel clearly stresses the solipsism of being-for-one: "though this moment has been designated as being-for-one, there is as yet nothing present for which it would be—no *one*" (*SL* 159); while everything is an object of my representation—and thus an extension of myself—*I* am not an object of anyone's representation. Even when I say that I am "one," this quality of mine exists only for *me:* "there is only *one* being-for-other, and because there is only one, this too is only a being-for-one" (ibid.). At this stage, then, being-for-one and being-for-self are "not genuinely opposed determinatenesses" and this is the reason why any talk about *a* being-for-self would be misleading (ibid.).

The next subsection is titled "The One" (*Eins*) and Hegel gives the reason for the subsection's unusual title: "Being-for-self is thus *a* being-for-self, and since in this immediacy its inner meaning vanishes, it is the wholly abstract limit of itself—the *one*" (*SL* 163). The sentence points to our present difficulty as well as to our first attempt to solve it. Being-for-self, we remember, turned out to be self-enclosed and so we were driven to view it as a "one." But being-for-self was not *a* one. Rather, it was the only one (the "Unique" as Max Stirner will call it soon, in a treatise in which the solipsism of the self will receive its most complete articulation). Such a one that is not *a* one, but the *only* one deserves to be called *the* one.

The tortuous path we shall now have to take in the section on "The One and the Many" can be smoothed somewhat if we continue to bear in mind the clues Hegel has offered us at the beginning of the whole chapter: we are dealing here all the time with a conceptual sequence which finds its full and complete embodiment in human self-consciousness. The present section too lays out a conceptual structure whose many sides are mirrored by various aspects of human self-consciousness. The complicated deduction of the dialectic of "The One and the Void" which now follows represents a conceptual reworking of what Hegel told us about self-consciousness in the *Phenomenology*: "when it [self-consciousness] distinguishes only its self as such from itself, distinction is straightway taken to be superseded in the sense of involving otherness. The distinction *is* not, and self-consciousness is only motionless tautology, Ego is Ego, I am I. When for self-consciousness the distinction does not also have a shape of *being*, it is *not* self-consciousness."[20] This long passage gives us several helpful indications on how to approach the corresponding section of the *Science of Logic*. This section—the section we are presently considering—brings out two important points. We learn, first of all, that in its emergence as a self-enclosed unit, the self is stripped of any specific content: as a "motionless tautology" the self is empty and indeterminate. In effect, our self-enclosed, solipsistic self knows no boundaries and no limits—everything falls within it, and this implies that in fact the self amounts to nothing, since (as we remember from the great triad) not being anything determinate amounts to being nothing at all. But—we are now being told in the second place—this empty relation of the self to (only) itself must also have "the shape of being," otherwise that relation is "*not* self-consciousness." We remember that self-consciousness (qua consciousness) must include a reference to its world; a self that is not defined by a relationship with the world is not a self at all. For Hegel, as for contemporary existentialists, the self is always a self-in-a-world. Thus even the abstract solipsistic self must be defined by some stand on what the world is like. In that world the solipsistic self finds only its own echo: this lonely, isolated self lives in a vacuum where it can encounter only itself. This self is an empty, hermetically closed realm, an "atom"—natural or social—devoid of any constitutive relations with other atoms; such is, in a nutshell, the conception deduced, explored, and overcome in the section on "The One and the Many."

The first subsection ("The One in its own self") conceptualizes the one in its first moment of the mere "motionless tautology," of the mere "Ego is Ego," as the *Phenomenology* put it. The one is now studied apart from its (inevitable and inevitably coming) dependency upon its world, upon what is outside the one. For the moment, the most that can be said about the one is that such a one is completely indeterminate and, for this reason, it represents a throwback to the pure indeterminate being (*SL* 164). On the other hand, however, the one is unlike the pure being, for the indeterminateness of the one is, nonetheless, the indeterminateness of a being-for-*self*; it is, therefore, the indeterminateness posited by the one itself (*SL* 164–65). Its emptiness and its solipsism, we may say, are all of the self's own making: we are analyzing an indeterminateness, but it is a self-induced and self-imposed indeterminateness. It is an indeterminateness nonetheless and, for this reason, it must pass over into nothing (just as the pure being passed over into pure nothing in the great triad). A being-for-self which absorbs everything, absorbs nothing in particular, ergo: it absorbs nothing at all, *nothing* (*SL* 164). This nothing is the quality of the one and—since we are still considering being-for-self—it is posited within the one (ibid.).

We recall though, that a self must be defined by a relationship to what lies outside it. Hence Hegel's next move (in the subsection "The One and the Void"): "as distinct from the affirmative being of the one, the nothing as the void is *outside* it" (*SL* 165).

Already in the first subsection Hegel was hinting at the premise
here taken for granted, for he told us then that for all its emptiness the one does have at least one "concrete determination"
(ibid.): the determination of being a being-for-*self*. This gave
the one a feature that the pure being did not yet have: a positive
and fulfilled ("affirmative") identity, the identity of being a self-
enclosed unit, unaffected by any outside influences and limits.
But having such an identity implies, for that self-enclosed unit
itself, the appropriate conception of the outside world (as, in
effect, deprived of any power to limit and to influence the self-
enclosed one). Now, an outside which fits the above description
is the void; for the void is precisely the sort of outside where the
one will find no limits and no constraints—it will find nothing
but itself.

There is still more to be learned from this subsection and,
again, Hegel's teaching becomes less esoteric if we constantly
keep in mind the key paradigm guiding his conceptualizations:
the human self-consciousness. A human self, for Hegel, is always a self-in-a-world. The self's identity is thus defined by its
world; but, at the same time—and quite plainly—the world is
not the self. Let us apply this to the relationship of the solipsistic
one to its own outside (the void). In the void the one finds only
itself (for, in effect, the void is the only outside where the one
can find nothing but itself), but the void is also *not* the one (for
the void is the external environment of the one). "The one and
the void have negative relation to self for their common, simple
base. The moments of being-for-self emerge from this unity,
become external to themselves" (*SL* 165). Since the one and the
void around it are thus set apart—the void has no internal
relation with *this* particular one any more—the void is construed as an indifferent medium (as empty physical or social
space) belonging to "no one in particular" and hence open to
many ones. We are at the stage of atomism—both in physical
and in social theory (*SL* 167, *Enc.* I, #98)—where natural and
social phenomena are explained in terms of mechanical interactions between independent basic units (material particles or
isolated human agents defined merely as strategic calculators of
self-interest).

It is obvious, though, that a step is still missing in this deduction. For even if the void ceases to be attached to this particular
one and thus becomes open to receive many other ones, no

argument has been offered, so far, as to why we are warranted in expecting the actual existence of those many ones. The next subsection ("Many Ones: Repulsion") is meant to answer this question.

The subsection makes the distinction between two senses of "repulsion." In one, and superficial, sense repulsion is simply a concept to be found—under so many different names—in any philosophy of atomism. In formulating an atomistic theory one is, inevitably, compelled to account for the individuality and discreteness of (physical or social) atoms. Thus a material particle may come to be viewed as endowed with a force of impenetrability, while a human individual may be thought of as endowed with a will which resists the encroachments of other individuals, etc. In this sense of "repulsion," the plurality of units is taken for granted: we assume that "there are" (or that there "must be" on hypothetical grounds, i.e., if we want to account for observable phenomena) such units in the universe, but we refrain from giving an intelligible account of the fact itself. This form of repulsion—the "second repulsion" as Hegel calls it, to stress its derivative and superficial status—"is what is immediately suggested to external reflexion: repulsion not as the *generation* of ones, but only as the mutual repelling of ones presupposed as already *present*" (*SL* 168). (The "external reflection" Hegel mentions in this passage is nothing other than the mode of thinking underlying the approach of modern science which constructs its account of the universe in terms of laws describing the behavior of material particles.) When taken in this way, the ones entertain no internal relations with each other. Each of them is a complete and completely self-enclosed unit and their interconnections boil down to contingent (although not lawless) encounters with other such units (hence the importance of the law of inertia: every particle remains in the same state unless acted upon from outside). If we then speak about a plurality of such units, we must not forget that the plurality in question "does not . . . concern the ones" (ibid.). In other words: that there are other ones cannot be deduced from the inner nature of this (or any other) particular one. The ones thus entertain a merely external relation and the medium of this relation—the void—reappears again at the end of Hegel's discussion of this ("second") form of repulsion (ibid.).

Now, the second repulsion presupposes what repulsion is "according to its Notion [as] repulsion *in itself*" (ibid.). Every student of Hegel will be familiar with the peculiarly Hegelian meaning of such a talk about the "in itself" or the "Notion" of this or that. We gain access to what an X is "in itself" or "according to its Notion" when (1) we grasp that X not in its superficial and partial aspects, but in its complete nature and when (2) we succeed in grasping these aspects as being derived from (and being manifestations of) the X's complete nature. Thus the second repulsion is the superficial and partial aspect of what repulsion is "according to its Notion"; and, further, the second repulsion is derived from that deeper—and complete—nature of repulsion. Only repulsion in its complete nature will supply us with an account of there being those many ones to begin with (this will be the derivation of what is merely presupposed by the second repulsion). And we will also learn in more detail why the second repulsion alone will not take us beyond the superficial and partial aspects of reality.

The bottom line of Hegel's argument is this: the one must *of itself* pass over into an other one; what the second repulsion takes for granted (the plurality of many ones) is in fact the finished product of a process, of a generation of many ones by each other. By focusing only upon the finished product, the second model of repulsion brings out only the external, fixed relations between the ones—and this is a superficial and limited conception which cannot sustain itself at least as a philosophical proposition (although Hegel was equally skeptical even of its scientific value).

The argument takes off, predictably, with a closer analysis of the results achieved in the preceding subsection ("The One and the Void"), prior to any talk about many ones. What we have deduced so far is, let us recall, the empty one on the one hand and the void on the other. There are important similarities and differences between them. "Each of these moments has a negation for its determination" (*SL* 167). Both the one and the void—both the self and the world, in Hegel's paradigm case— are not merely given items; rather they are the empty frameworks, within which any such items (contents of the self's life on the one hand and the furniture of the world on the other hand) would have to be arranged. Furthermore, Hegel informs us in the next part of the same sentence, even as such "negations" each of these two moments "is at the same time posited as a determinate being" (ibid.). The self is still the self, while the world is still the world. But this raises, immediately, the following difficulty. If the two moments are equally determined as "negations," then on what grounds do we distinguish between the negation as the self (the one) and the same negation as the world (the void)? Given the poverty and the abstractness of the conceptual resources at our disposal we can only answer the question by saying that the first negation is the one and the second negation is the void; but, Hegel points out, since the only meaning we can attribute to these two conceptions (the one and the void) is the same in both cases (mere negation, emptiness), the one and the void are indistinguishable: "the one is essentially self-relation only as related *negation,* that is, it is itself that which the void outside it is supposed to be" (*SL* 167). Again, we have failed to articulate the distinction between the one and the void. However, we have at least become clear as to what is now required. The one needs to be set in contrast with an outside which, its emptiness notwithstanding, must be a quite specific, concrete entity and not simply "an unspecified determinate being in general" (as was the void). What could fit the description Hegel has prepared? Only "as essentially *self*-relation, the other is not indeterminate negation as the void, but is likewise a *one*. The one is consequently a *becoming of many ones*" (*SL* 167).

What are we to make of this abstract dialectic? It seems to me that, once again, we should follow closely the clues Hegel has given us at the very beginning of the chapter: the category of being-for-self finds its full and complete realization in human self-consciousness. Hegel's abstract deduction of the many from the one—for this is indeed what is here at stake (*Enc.* I, #97)— becomes more intelligible when we shift back to Hegel's paradigm case: to the relation of a (human) self to other selves. Let us look more closely. A human self as we ought to consider it here (i.e., in conformity with the present complexity of being-for-self) must be (1) an *empty* self, a mere I am I and (2) a *particular* self (as indicated by our very use of the personal pronoun). Now we remember from our previous discussion that an empty, vacuous self must be defined by a relation to an empty, vacuous outside. But such an empty, vacuous outside can establish the self as a particular self (as *this* self) only if this outside is itself another self. Plainly and obviously, I can describe myself as this particular self only if I think of (and contrast myself with) other such selves. Given the resources of the present conceptual stage, those other selves, too, can only be seen as vacuous—but they are still seen as distinct from my own self. Thus my self implies other selves by its very inner nature; and, in this sense, self-consciousness will "pass over" into another self-consciousness in exactly the same way as the logical one will pass over into another logical one. Hegel's terms in the *Phenomenology* are unmistakable: "self-consciousness has before it another self-consciousness; *it has come outside itself.*"[21] The same thought, in wording even more closely related to that of the *Science of Logic,* can be found in the *Encyclopaedia*'s section on the *Phenomenology (Enc.* III, ##429–30).

The one is the becoming of many ones, but (*SL* 167) since the entire transition is not a play of the indeterminate being and nothing, but the setting up by the one of the many ones as existing outside it, the transition may well be called a "repulsion"—and, this time, it is the repulsion in its essential nature, i.e., as the process of generating the multiplicity of ones. In contrast, the "second repulsion"—the notion of repulsion as it is employed in atomism—glosses over that internal, dynamic connection of the ones: "As an explication of what the one is in itself, the becoming of the many, or the generation of the many, vanishes immediately; the products of the process are ones, and these are not for an other, but relate themselves infinitely to themselves" (*SL* 168). A superficial and distorted view of repulsion has come to dominate our thinking.

Hence the contradiction that Hegel will bring out in the final sentences of the present subsection (*SL* 169). According to the first notion of repulsion, the ones entertain an internal relation with each other. When we posit the (allegedly) only one, this one breaks out of its isolation and shows itself to be, by a necessity of its nature, a one among many. "In other words, the plurality of the one is of its own positing" (ibid.). This is the first proposition. But, second, on the model of our superficial and derivative repulsion, the one is construed as stripped of any necessary connection with other ones: "plurality is absolutely external to the one" (ibid.). It is easy to see that those two propositions are in conflict with each other: the connection with the many is posited, in the same breath, as both necessary and contingent to the one. In order to illustrate the difficulty Hegel takes up again (ibid.) the case of Leibniz. From Hegel's point of view such a lumping together of Leibniz with atomism—Leibniz's position being here interpreted as the most extreme version of atomism—is quite correct and quite in line with Hegel's earlier use of Leibniz's philosophy. For Leibniz has discovered not only—as we were already told by Hegel—the notion of being-for-self but, in addition, he has attributed to this being-for-self the determination of a one, of a self-enclosed unit (a monad). When taken merely in this status of a self-enclosed unit, the Leibnizian monad is indeed, and on Leibniz's own authority, an "atom."[22] No interaction whatever is then possible between the monads, and so the unity of the world has to be reconstructed from the notion of a preestablished harmony (and this notion, whatever its merits in comparison to occasionalism, still fails to account for the inner necessity of the connection between monads). The cause of Leibniz's failure is identical with the main shortcoming of atomism in general: Leibniz "takes up the plurality as something *given* and does not grasp it as a *repulsion* of the monads" (ibid.).

The need for repulsion—for repulsion as the internal relation of the one with the many (*Enc.* I, #95, Zusatz), not for that superficial "second repulsion," where the self-enclosed units exist in total indifference towards each other—is thus asserting itself again. But—and this is the new element in our conceptual situation—we are now at a stage *past* the original repulsion (repulsion "according to its Notion") and its setting into a plurality of ones. Thus the new repulsion—the repulsion reestablishing the internal connection between one one and other ones—will occur given the background of an already existing plurality of ones. Hegel calls this new (third) form of repulsion "Exclusion." Fortunately, we need not engage in any guesswork in order to discover the paradigm underlying Hegel's analyses of repulsion as exclusion. Hegel intends to keep nothing secret from us: "It is the supreme, most stubborn error, which takes itself for the highest truth, manifesting in more concrete forms as abstract freedom, pure Ego, and further, Evil" (*SL* 172). This sentence appears in a "Remark" following the subsection on exclusion, and it offers an explanation of what Hegel's analysis of exclusion was meant to conceptualize in the first place: certain quite definite *human attitudes* which are identified in plain terms. A one which "excludes" other ones is an "evil" human self setting itself apart from and against the community of other selves—apart from and against its own community. Such ("abstract") use of human freedom is precisely what Hegel identifies as the source of evil. It is the sort of freedom where a human self refuses to think and act as a member of the community; the sort of freedom where an individual, instead of guiding his conduct by a set of public rules and obligations, considers his own private self as the repository of truth and value.

The exclusive, evil self is also "vain" and "proud". This is how the exclusive self is described in those parts of the *Philosophy of Religion*[23] which cover the same ground as does the present section in the *Science of Logic*. We cannot here enter the complicated issue of how to properly understand the relationship between religion and philosophy (identity in content, but difference in form—representational in religion, conceptual in philosophy). Let us only note that even in his merely logical treatment of the notion of infinity Hegel does not miss the chance to tell us (*SL* 155) that philosophy and religion are both concerned with that notion, and that its development in logic follows the same path as does its ("representational") development in religion.[24] Finally, the result of the self's "vain" and "proud" attitudes are human "enmity, hatred and contempt"[25] that is, the forces generating violence.[26]

This human, anthropological context supplies not only the paradigm of Hegel's treatment of exclusion, but it also makes intelligible the specific tension which sets exclusion in motion. This tension I shall now spell out both in its merely logical terms and in its underlying human paradigm as Hegel was aware of it beginning at least with his Jena system.[27]

The "second repulsion," we remember, was a distortion of the repulsion "according to its Notion." For what is implied by the notion of repulsion (and what was ignored by the second repulsion) is the *communal* status of the one: the (allegedly) "only one" is constituted by its relations with other ones. The model of second repulsion has severed that bond—that *continuity,* Hegel will soon say—of a one with other ones. This model has isolated a one by making an "atom" out of it. The other ones are now indifferent and external to our initial one. As far as the latter is concerned, the very existence of those other ones is a matter of mere contingency and givenness.

A new contradiction is about to emerge. Since a self-enclosed one is, not only for us but also for itself, an "entire closed universe" (*SL* 169), it can tolerate nothing that would limit it from outside as an alien, foreign presence. Thus the brute presence of other ones (in conformity with the model of second repulsion) is an unbearable challenge to the self-image of the one. The one's claim is to exclusivity (i.e., to be that "entire closed universe") and so the one has no alternative but to exclude (i.e., to destroy, to annihilate) other ones: "Thus repulsion now simply *finds immediately before* it that which is repelled by it. In this determination repulsion is an *exclusion;* the one repels from itself only the many ones which are neither generated nor posited by it" (*SL* 170).

We must now supplement this understanding of exclusion as seen from within the perspective of a particular one with our own—higher and more complete—understanding of it. For we know that exclusion is a "mutual repulsion" (ibid.); we know not only that there are many ones but that, in addition, *every* one sees the others as an unbearable challenge and thus sets out to destroy them. Hence each and every one appears to us as, we may say, equally "narcissistic" in its drive to impose its rule upon the world. But this equality of their predicament has not yet dawned upon the ones themselves.

The one bent on merely excluding the other ones is, we saw, a "vain" and an "evil" one. Whatever one may think of Hegel's *naturphilosophisch* uses of the notions of attraction and repulsion,[28] it is clear that a natural force cannot be called "evil" or "vain." The proper testing ground of Hegel's conceptual grid is to be found in the area of *human* relations.

In anticipation of Hegel's forthcoming deduction of attraction from repulsion (i.e., of community from violent struggle) we must now ask the following question. If the emergence of community is preceded by the violent struggle of the antagonistic ones, then just where are we to locate such a struggle in the (paradigm) case of the human combatants? This question confronts us with a serious paradox in Hegel's account.

On the one hand, it seems clear that it would be a mistake to situate the struggle where Hobbes originally saw it: in the state of nature. For, on Hegel's account, no talk about freedom in the state of nature is warranted[29]—and the same must be said, even more strongly, about any talk of "evil" and of "pure ego" in the state of nature—while the violence of exclusion means an attitude in which the freedom of the self is said to find *some* ("abstract", etc.) form of expression. Since freedom can only be attributed to a *social* man[30] we must conclude that the violence unleashed by a self bent on excluding other selves must be viewed as an attitude of an eminently social man.

On the other hand, we can *not* view the struggle in this way. For in the violence of exclusion, the purpose of the agent is nothing other than the destruction of his community and of his own status as a communal being. In annihilating his adversaries through the blind, unrestricted violence of exclusion, the individual does not aim at boosting his image or his standing among his peers, but at wiping out any independent others altogether. This truly exclusive character of exclusion cannot be over-emphasized. Here the violent self does not destroy his adversary in order to gain the admiration of someone he respects—of a third self or of a fourth, and so on. Since any independent onlooker could only be himself just another threat to the self's narcissistic claim, he too must be annihilated. The violence against the other reaches the other *as other,* and it thus applies to all independent others. A successful completion of exclusion would leave the self all alone; and to those who would want to claim that such a self would still be social at least "in principle" if not "in fact" one would have to reply that, for Hegel, a principle severed from any facts is not a principle but an empty thought, a fiction. An action which aims at the sheer annihilation of (any and all) independent others is not itself an action of a social man but, rather, the sort of action which is dedicated to the destruction of the social realm as such.

The paradox emerging from Hegel's theory of violence as exclusion is, then, as follows. On the one hand, this form of violence is unleashed by a "free" self asserting unconditionally its "vanity" and its "evil"; the violence, therefore, originates in and as a social attitude of a social man (for this reason, exclusion could not erupt in the state of nature). On the other hand, this form of violence aims at a purpose which amounts to the destruction of the social realm as such (for this reason, exclusion cannot be just another social attitude). The conclusion is inevitable: we must accept a form of violence in which the already socialized and social man turns against his own status as a social being. By doing this, however, man turns against and destroys, what is, in effect, his own essence: "this self-subsistence [of the exclusive self] is the error of regarding as negative that which is *its own essence* and of adopting a negative attitude towards it" (*SL* 172; my emphasis). The very same point is driven home in the *Philosophy of Religion*.[31]

We are now in a position to advance a further claim. Just as the impulse towards exclusion is based on a free repudiation, by man, of his status as a communal being, so too the repudiation of this repudiation—through man's acknowledgment of community—is also due to his own action and commitment: "it is only the *letting go* of the negativity of its being-for-self instead of holding fast to it" (ibid.). Now, if man's acknowledgment of community must thus express his own free commitment, then the path of abstract freedom—and hence also the path of violence—must remain an ever-present option to him. Without this option, man would be enclosed by nature within a community and he could not, in effect, establish himself as a free being.

We have seen the seeds of this idea already in Kant's treatment of the purely theoretical concept of freedom in the Third Antinomy. For that concept to make sense, Kant argued, we must attribute to the agent not only the capacity to choose and act independently of any *causes*, but also the capacity to choose and act independently of any *reasons*. For unless we attribute to the agent precisely such a capacity to not follow up on any reasons to act, then those reasons will be transformed into quasi-natural laws and freedom will thus become "nature under another name" (*CPR*, A447, B475)—it will become a natural quality of human agency. Freedom must thus preserve the option of denying (even) its own law—and since the law of freedom (the categorical imperative) commands respect for human community, a truly free agent must preserve the option of turning against his status as a communal being and of thus choosing the path of evil.

The idea, the argument, even the wording are all to be found in Hegel as well. While, says Hegel, "planets, plants and animals cannot deviate from the necessity of their nature," the freedom of man, *not being man's nature,* gives him the option of denying his own true destiny qua rational, communal being.[32] This destiny remains, to be sure, man's "necessity and truth," but, at the same time, man would not be entitled to consider himself free unless he had the capacity to break away both from his "truth" and his "necessity." And only by exercising this capacity—only by becoming evil—does man rise to the level of being-for-self: "To be evil means in an abstract sense to isolate myself. . . . But it is along with this separation that Being-for-self originates, and it is only when it appears that we have the spiritual as something universal, as Law, what ought to be."[33]

While in the *Philosophy of Religion* the idea of the abstract, negative freedom—exemplified by the story of the Fall[34]—is studied as a rebellion against God and God's law, we must not forget that in God man finds his own Essence[35]—and that means also (and even above all) his essence as a communal being. Thus the negative freedom can also be represented in a secularized fashion, as man's repudiation of all laws and values making possible a human community. And this is exactly how Hegel represents the negative freedom in the Introduction to his *Philosophy of Right.* The pure, isolated ego sets itself apart from and against every ethical content; and this "freedom of the void" can aim at nothing short of "the destruction of the whole subsisting social order . . . and the annihilation of any organization which tries to arise anew from the ruins."[36] This freedom spends itself in a "fury of destruction";[37] and this fury aims not at rebuilding the human community (be it even under different laws and values), but at destroying it altogether.

For the intelligibility of the next stage we must return, as Hegel instructs us, to the purely *logical* development of being-for-self.[38] We are at the end of the stage of exclusion. At this necessary and inevitable stage a single one reaches the full depth of its particularity and separateness by unleashing its violence against the community of other ones. But then how can any acknowledgment of that community emerge from the perspective of an exclusive one?

To answer this question we must follow the movement through which repulsion—in its final, exclusive stage—turns into attraction. The movement will take place, Hegel thinks, as soon as the exclusive one discovers the *commonality of predicament* binding it with other ones. Every exclusive one will thus find itself as being only a one among others—a member of a community—and this discovery, Hegel says, will concern both the ones' mere being as well as their mutual positing through the negation of their being (*SL* 171).

Hegel first considers the ones from his own point of view—from the point of view of the philosopher as he grasps, from his ultimate perspective, the hidden presuppositions of the present stage. The two aspects in which the merely exclusive one must pass over into attraction stand out immediately. First, the being (the reality) of a one is what allows this one to withstand the exclusive drive directed at it by other ones. In effect, if the one succumbs to such a drive, then it *is* no longer; its being depends upon its ability to resist other ones. But its being has been, in addition, determined as a self-enclosed unit, a one. Thus the one preserves its being when it succeeds in maintaining itself and in maintaining itself *as* one (ibid.). But this can be said about each and every one; it can be said of all of them: "*this is what they are all*; they are in their being-in-itself the *same*" (ibid.). In the second place, the ones are all alike not only in their being but in the negation of their being as well. The ones are, and they negate each other's being through the exclusive drive. They are all alike in their being and they are also all alike in their exclusive drive (in their "negation of being"), since each and every one of them pursues the annihilation of others. We thus discover the sameness of the ones' predicament both as far as their being and their being's negation are concerned: "their *positing themselves as ones,* is the reciprocal negating of themselves; but this likewise is *one and the same* determination of them all; through which they then rather posit themselves as identical" (ibid.). In exploring the (extreme) repulsion of the ones we thus hit upon their attraction. The ones must be viewed as standing within a "*one* affirmative unity" (ibid.), since the sameness of both their being and their (negative) relation to their being makes it necessary to conceive them as endowed with a *shared, common identity.*

We have not gone, so far, beyond "a comparison made by us" (ibid.) as we consider the ones from our own (and higher) point of view, with a clear grasp of the hidden presuppositions underlying the stage of pure exclusion. From now on we shall be considering the emergence of these presuppositions from within the perspective of the ones themselves. Let us observe closely what emerges from their own "inter-relatedness" (*SL* 171).[39] We observe, first, that for every one its own reality, its *being*, can be secured only insofar as the one escapes the exclusive, annihilating drive of other ones. The one *is* if it succeeds in negating the other ones (which are trying to negate it); and the one would immediately cease to be if it were destroyed by the negation—by the violence of exclusion—directed at it by other ones.[40] But the being of ones is not an unknowable *X*; we have seen long ago that being and its identity (determinateness) cannot be set apart; we have seen that an entity cannot be without being *as* something or other. We also know the identity of the entity we are now analyzing: our one exists *as* clashing with other ones in the battle of mutual exclusion. A contradiction arises at once. Every one can exist only insofar as it resists the exclusive drive of other ones. But (1) such a resistance puts a quick end to the initial narcissistic identity that every one attributed to itself. Every one finds out that there is a reality "out there" which it cannot dominate and which threatens it. Thus (2) the ones' very being is threatened.[41] Wouldn't it at least be possible to think—Hegel asks rhetorically—that a one educated out of its narcissism by the resistance of other ones may still preserve its being even while shedding its self-conception of a self-enclosed unit?[42] The answer is no, since being is here determinate being, and so a one can only be if it preserves itself as a self-enclosed unit; but a one cannot preserve itself as such a self-enclosed unit unless it carries out successfully its program of exterminating its adversaries.[43] Since the entire operation is eminently *un*successful, the ones lose their identity and—as their very existence depended upon the preservation of that identity—they "do not preserve themselves, and so are not" (*SL* 171).

Due to this sudden turn of their fate, however, the ones also discover their common predicament. They discover that they are not different at all—on the contrary, they are all equally violent and equally vulnerable. This mutual realization of their common identity allows them to gain a conception of themselves as members of a community, of a "single one" (*SL* 172) which represents the bond that holds them together. This bond between them cannot be thought of as membership in a class to which they would all be assigned due to possession of certain marks and features. The bond is an internal one: it is the acknowledged kinship of all the ones, a "going-together-with-self" (*Mit-sich-zusammengehen*). Feuerbach and Marx will soon borrow heavily from this conception by describing man as a "species being" (*Gattungwesen*). Hegel's logical category for this acknowledged commonality of ones is "attraction." More exactly, the plurality of ones is drawn together ("attracted") into a single community: into "The one One of Attraction," as Hegel puts it in the title of the next subsection.

Paradoxically, this coalescence of the ones within a community fulfills their own striving even as it frustrates its crude narcissistic form. Thus our earlier statements must be severely amended and qualified. In becoming a member of a community, the exclusive one, to be sure, loses itself—but it also finds itself. Let us pay closer attention to this point. Since the exclusive relation of the ones to each other is, Hegel reminds us, "without effect" (*SL* 173)—for every one resists the encroachments of other ones and thereby frustrates their narcissism—the aim of repulsion is but a pipe dream, an unachievable task. The repelling one aims at purging its outside from all foreign and alien elements, but the ideality of the one cannot successfully absorb the entire outward reality: such aim of the one "is only the ought-to-be of ideality" (ibid.). In attraction, however, this imperative of the one to "idealize" reality—i.e., to bring reality within its own sphere—fulfills itself (ibid.). For while it cannot be denied that the one *A* is *not* the one *B*—or *C*, or *D*, etc.—it is also clear that *B* has by now lost the status of something alien and foreign to *A*. For *A*, *B* is now a *kin*, an extension of *A* itself. In accepting to *belong* with *B*, *A* ceases to consider *B* as a violation of its own identity; rather, *A*'s identity is now confirmed and strengthened by being externalized in its *fellow B*.

Whereas repulsion fulfills itself in attraction, attraction in turn presupposes repulsion. A community is a community of individuals; and this requires that individuals first establish themselves as particular selves. The requirement cannot be met otherwise than through repulsion (*SL* 173). The repulsion at issue is here, invariably, exclusion. Exclusion, in turn, is violence. It follows that the establishment of individuals qua particular selves demands violence. We shall soon return to this important theme.

Let us note, in the meantime, that the attraction we have just witnessed emerging from exclusion represents the second—and mediated—stage of attraction. As we recall, even prior to the violence of exclusion the one was not the only one but, rather, a one among many—an atom among atoms. Every one thus found itself surrounded by many. Their interconnectedness was merely external and lacked any inner necessity; but, nevertheless, even then the ones had to be posited as interacting somehow (even from a preestablished harmony) and thus as brought together in a community. But that community, we must also recall, was imposed upon the ones from outside: *they* did not sublate their separateness. That sublation was achieved only further down the road, through the meanders of exclusion. Prior to exclusion, then, the attraction of the ones is not anchored in the ones themselves: "rather is attraction the positing of the immediately present indifferentiatedness of the ones" (*SL* 174) coexisting alongside each other in the void. In contrast, the attraction resulting from the recent test of violence is a mediated attraction: the ones have first broken out of their indifferent coexistence by setting themselves apart in violence and they have then acknowledged their belonging-together within a community posited through their own actions—through the actions of each and every particular one. The "one One of Attraction"—the community as we consider it in the present subsection—is thus "realized ideality posited in the one" (ibid.). The aspiration of the one to "idealize" its outside—the aspiration to purge the outside of any elements foreign and alien to the one; the aspiration to bring the outside within the identity of the one—is now fulfilled, since the community is the one's own community, the community where the one *belongs*. And as this belonging is also mediated by exclusion—for prior to drawing together in a community the ones opposed each other in violence—the distinctness of every member of the community is preserved. They belong together, but they do so as distinct selves; the community "does not absorb the attracted ones into itself as into a center . . . it does not sublate them abstractly" (ibid.). For there to *be* any individuals qua distinct selves—and not simply qua anonymous materials swallowed up, as if in an anthill, by the community—repulsion must be preserved in attraction (ibid.); there must be a unity of attraction and repulsion (ibid.).

The task of grasping the principle of this unity sets off our thinking onto the next stages of its journey. The important subsection "The Relation of Repulsion and Attraction" will zero in on that principle and, in the process of doing so, will lead our thinking from the category of quality to that of quantity.

The subsection begins with a broad overview of the terrain we have covered thus far in our study of repulsion and attraction. In the first stages of our journey, repulsion and attraction were set apart. Then we saw them coming together through the unfolding of exclusion, where the excluding ones proved to be subject to attraction as well. It thus turned out that, in the end, we could not sustain our initial view attributing to repulsion priority over attraction; repulsion, we were driven to conclude, must presuppose attraction just as much as attraction presupposes repulsion. The restatement of this conclusion (*SL* 175) gives rise to a new difficulty which is due to our inability to think through what is in fact included in the conclusion. We say that attraction "presupposes" repulsion and vice versa. We thus imply that attraction and repulsion, albeit working jointly, are two qualitatively different—indeed qualitatively opposite—forces. A paradox arises: attraction and repulsion "as thus determined are inseparable and at the same time each is determined as an ought and a limitation relatively to the other" (ibid.). Attraction is *not* repulsion; repulsion is *not* attraction; each is a "different determining" (ibid.); attraction is only the positing of community, repulsion is only the splitting of community into individuals. This is why, as Hegel just told us, they are a mere "limitation" of each other: each is beyond the boundaries, beyond the proper area of the other. And this is also why we are told that they are an "ought" to each other. In order to better understand this last claim we must recall what we have learned from Hegel's main criticism of the ought (*Sollen*). The contradiction of the ought is as follows. If we say that *A* ought to become *B,* we imply both (1) that no such feat will ever actually take place (thus attraction as we have just thought it out will never merge with repulsion) and (2) that such a feat

is nevertheless necessary. Now, why is the merger of attraction
with repulsion necessary? Its necessity is implied even by our
present crude model of attraction and repulsion. We said that
they "presuppose" each other. If so, they should not be
thought of as those qualitatively "different determinings" we
have just thought them to be. If repulsion is necessary for there
to be any attraction and if attraction is necessary for there to be
any repulsion, then attraction and repulsion must be thought
as moments of a broader unity. Within that unity repulsion is
not an external presupposition of attraction; repulsion is attraction's own "*self*-presupposing," just as, conversely,
attraction is the "self-presupposing" of repulsion (*SL* 176).
But attraction, we remember, is the drawing together of the
many ones into a community, while repulsion secures the individuality of these ones. Since repulsion is now the inner
unfolding (self-presupposing) of attraction—and conversely—
the relation between individuals and community becomes now
truly internal: "The one as such, then, is a coming-out-of-itself,
is only the positing of itself as its own other, as many; and the
many, similarly, is only this, to collapse within itself and to
posit itself as *its* other, as one, and in this very act to be related
only to its own self, each continuing itself in its other" (ibid.).

We now stand at the threshold of quantity, indeed we have
reached quantity already, for when repulsion shows itself to be
attraction as well, the "Being-for-self suppresses itself" (*Enc.* I,
#98) and the conception of a qualitative unit—of a unit distin-
guishable, by its inner quality, from everything else—yields
place to the conception of *different,* but *qualitatively indistinguishable* units (*SL* 177), i.e., to the conception of quantity
(*Enc.* I, #98). The transition from quality to quantity, we can
notice at once, is accomplished by the leveling down of qualitative contrasts and differences. A qualitatively determined one
was at first posited as repelling another qualitatively determined
one. We have just seen, however, that as members of the same
"one one" (i.e., of the same community to which they belong)
the ones are all *alike.* They are thus (if only in this respect)
qualitatively indistinguishable; their difference is conjoined
with their qualitative sameness. But the difference of identicals
(i.e., of such items as are qualitatively indiscernible) is nothing
other than quantity (for example, two perfectly identical twins
can only be distinguished numerically, etc.).

Hegel now offers us a "brief survey of the moments of this *transition of quality*" (*SL* 177). This "survey" can best be described as a way of bringing out a broad general contrast between quality and quantity. The contrast is both simple and fundamental to the opposition of quantity and quality. As long as we remain within the categories of quality, every "one" is endowed with the sort of determinateness which cannot be stretched beyond certain limits without destroying that one's identity—and hence also the one's being. Changes in quantity, however, do not destroy the identity of the thing in question. In quantity, "the one . . . is posited as the limit which is no limit, which is present in being but is indifferent to it" (*SL* 178). For example (*Enc.* I, #99), a house does not cease to be a house whether its size increases or diminishes.

The section on "Repulsion and Attraction" concludes with a "Remark" titled "The Kantian Construction of Matter from the Forces of Attraction and Repulsion." This Remark calls for a commentary of its own.[44]

Conclusion: Violence and Community

The key notions of philosophy, we remember from our motto, converge in the category of being-for-self. With the emergence of the identity of repulsion and attraction "the development of being-for-self is completed and has reached its conclusion" (*SL* 177). Our reflection upon this conclusion yields a new category: quantity. For the purposes of the present study, however, we need only consider that unity of attraction and repulsion as the term of the development of being-for-self. These two ways of looking at the attraction-repulsion unity—i.e., either as a new category in its own right or as the term of the prior categorial development—are not at all identical. Hence the differences of emphasis in Hegel's own expressions: in the unity of attraction and repulsion the being-for-self is said to suppress itself (*Enc.* I, #98), but this very same unity is also the completion of being-for-self's development (*SL* 177). It is from this second angle that we shall now approach the unity of repulsion and attraction.

We must note, to begin with, that in the process of carrying out the violence of exclusion the one has discovered itself as a *particular* one. To be sure, even prior to the violence of exclusion the one found itself to be a "one among many." But that thought vanished quickly due to the one's stubborn pretension to be a self-enclosed, all-encompassing unit. The one thought itself free to deny the reality of other ones. Violence alone was able to (brutally) persuade the one that the whole world was not its own private domain. Let us think again about Hegel's paradigm case—the *human* case. In discovering the "resistance" (*Widerstand* [SL 171]) of my adversaries during the struggle, I am brought face to face with my limits: there is a power (like my own but appearing outside me) which escapes my violence and which poses a threat to my entire being. Contrary to my initial narcissistic assumption I do not encompass all of being within my boundaries—violence educates me to the inescapable reality of others; and so I finally begin to view myself as being only one particular self among other selves.

Violence too is the necessary condition of my emergence as a universal, communal being. For to rise to the level of universality I must, first, gain a perspective broader than, and independent of, my particular self; and I do gain such a perspective precisely insofar as I discover—due to a threat of violence—that this self is not "all there is" and that, therefore, reality cannot be measured by my own particular beliefs and values.[45] The second step required for my emergence as a universal self is also due to violence. In order to establish myself as such a universal self I must not only break the bond binding me with my particular self but I must also identify with the other's (the public) point of view. This identification is the first outcome of the struggle: the predicament that I am in is the predicament that the other is in, and we are brought together due to a common experience of violence. We are both equally violent and equally vulnerable, and the predicament we thus share creates a common frame of reference, a common point of view. I can now see myself as he sees me and he can see himself as I see him. And this means that I am not locked within my own particular perspective any more: I can envision things from the point of view of others; I rise to the level of a universal self.

Since my particular self is what gives my life its entire content and since my perspective is now not defined by my particular self, I can abstract from that whole content; I am thus able to take nothing for granted. I can now suspend my naive, uncritical attachment to the beliefs and attitudes defining my particular self. The path of withdrawal from the entire ordinary attitude—defined by those beliefs and attitudes—is now open to me.

But this was precisely what was required to open up the great triad. The pure being was thought up only thanks to my ability not to take for granted my immediate, untested conceptions. The pure being was only the "absolute poverty" (the nothing) of a total withdrawal from all content. We now see that it is the other's violence which renders me so thoroughly destitute. I can count on *nothing* to erase my vulnerability to him and hence my entire life—with all the goods, ties, and beliefs that sustain it—ceases to be taken for granted. This puts me in a position to make the logical beginning and to begin philosophizing; provided, of course, that my finitude and vulnerability are comprehended and articulated within that "mood of indifference" which, Hegel told us, creates the only environment where philosophy can grow.

Naturally, the logical beginning is also public. It does not represent a particular self's subjective certainty (*Gewissheit*), but the minimum of Logos. We may disagree on everything particular, but in so disagreeing we agree at least on the conception of pure being. In spite of its poverty, pure being is still universal. Hence if I am to grasp it, I must be a universal, public self. And for this too violence, if not sufficient, is at least necessary—for I can find common ground with the other only insofar as both of us can endure the mortal danger of the struggle and can thus think independently of a blind attachment to our particular selves. This is why attraction had to be preceded by exclusion. To conclude: both violence and community are required if we are to account for the sort of self capable of thinking the great triad and hence also its further developments in the unfolding circle of pure Logos.

Given Hegel's rationalistic framework, however, it becomes altogether impossible to account for that relationship of community and violence. In conclusion to his main argument Hegel writes: "It directly follows from this comparison of the many with one another that any one is determined simply like any other one; each is one, each is one of the many, *is* by excluding the others—so that they are absolutely the same, there is present one and only one determination. This is the *fact*, and all that has

146   HEGEL: LOGOS AND VIOLENCE

to be done is to grasp this simple fact" (*SL* 172–73). This
passage conveys quite well the fundamental difficulty implied by
Hegel's position. As soon as the warring individuals stop and
think (as soon as they carry out that "comparison" of their
standing vis-à-vis each other) violence must come to an end, for
it appears to them as entirely counterproductive—instead of
asserting his difference and uniqueness, each individual finds
himself doing exactly the same thing as the others; and so instead of finding his own unique identity he loses himself in the
crowd. Violence—or at least the blind, unconditional violence
of exclusion—now ceases to make any sense. And yet, Hegel
taught, it is precisely due to the possibility of this form of violence (pursued by an "evil" human self, filled only with "vanity"
and "pride") that man's status as a member of a community is
not a nature to him. The possibility of turning against the
community—against *any* human community—and thus also
against his own essence as a communal being remains the very
condition of man's capacity to commit himself freely to that
community. And even if we were prepared to grant that in order
to keep that capacity alive, an individual does not have to actually engage in acts of violent rebellion, it would still be required
that the path of such blind violence remain at least a viable,
meaningful option to an individual. But even this is out of the
question now, since a thinking individual cannot fail to see that
path as a plunge into anonymity and sameness.

   When Hegel does try to give an account of a thinking self's
option for violence—when violence erupts during the struggle
for recognition (*Anerkennung*)—such form of violence is, in
fact, a ritualized social game and the killing of one's adversary is
due only to an accident.

   It is highly significant that throughout the entire analysis of
violence in the *Science of Logic* not even a verbal reference is made
to the struggle for recognition—this is in spite of Hegel's belief
in that grand scheme of things in which the logical unfolding of
the categories is supposed to correspond to the experiential
development in the *Phenomenology of Spirit* (where the struggle
is precisely the struggle for recognition). Here, then, is one clear
case where such correspondence is not to be found. In exclusion, an individual sets out to annihilate the other qua other; the

destructive impulse is truly unconditional and is set off by the mere presence of the other. In recognition the battle erupts—if it can erupt at all—only because it is meant to serve as a medium of communication with the other, as a way of allowing one-self—and the adversary—to emerge in the status of free and independent self-consciousness. For in order to reach that status, a human agent must be able to show a greater attachment to honor and dignity than to life and security; and the struggle for recognition is meant to give to the individuals an opportunity to thus establish themselves as independent of a slavish attachment to life.

The main "contradiction"—this is Hegel's own word (*Enc.* III, #431, Zusatz)—that sets off the struggle for recognition is as follows. On the one hand both I and the other self encountered by me are perceived as mere *natural* beings, determined by impulse, need, instinct of self-preservation, etc. This is how *I* see myself and the other, this is how *he* sees me and himself. On the other hand, each of us has a conception of both himself and his adversary which is incompatible with the first view: for each of us sees himself and the other as not just mere beings of crude need and instinct but as genuinely free selves. The struggle for recognition is meant to resolve that contradiction. By battling the other for my honor I show that my instinct of self-preservation does not hold me in its grip; and I show this to an adversary capable of a similar victory over his own blind attachment to life—to an adversary, that is, whose recognition of my courage can be taken seriously due to the courage *he* has displayed during the struggle.

Thus the struggle for recognition is guided and sustained by a *communicative intention*. But one cannot communicate with a corpse. And so the death of one's adversary—not to mention one's own—is actually incompatible with the aim of the struggle for recognition. How, then, are we to conceive that struggle? Hegel could not be clearer on this point: "The fight for recognition is a life and death struggle: either self-consciousness imperils the other's life, and incurs a like peril for its own—but only peril, for either is no less bent on maintaining his life, as the existence of his freedom. Thus the death of one . . . is . . . from the essential point of view (i.e., the outward and visible recogni-

tion) a new contradiction (for that recognition is at the same
time undone by the other's death) and a greater than the other"
(*Enc.* III, #432).

No extended commentary is needed, in the light of this statement of Hegel's, to measure the distance separating the (ritualized) fight for recognition from the blind violence of exclusion.
When entering the struggle for recognition I must, to be sure,
reach out for a freedom and an independence which can come
only from my readiness to imperil my (and the other's) life—but
I must also stop at the brink, since death (either my own or my
adversary's) is incompatible with the very purpose of the struggle. The purpose was, from the very beginning, to validate
myself (as a free, but also living self) in the eyes of the other (as a
free but also living self). Thus the struggle must be carefully
staged and controlled; death can only result from an accident.
This is why the purposes of recognition can be fully reached
without violence—by achievement of honors and positions
within a state (*Enc.* III, #432, Zusatz). In contrast, the violence
of exclusion is unleashed by that "evil" individual who does not
pursue honors within a community but turns against it—and
hence also against himself as a communal being. Now, the continuity between the purpose of the struggle for recognition and
the pursuit of honors within a community is itself the best
indication of the inherently social and communal quality of the
struggle for recognition: violence, here, is meant to be played
out against the background of a bond uniting the warring individuals, and thus against the background of their mutual need
for each other.

Such a need, we remember, was missing in the violence of
exclusion. Yet exclusion, Hegel argued in the *Science of Logic,* is
the necessary and inevitable stage in the establishment of a one
qua one—i.e., in its capacity of a self capable of standing on its
own, apart from all its communal ties and attachments. This is
why, too, the path of the abstract freedom—of the freedom to
deny and to repudiate one's belonging to a community—must
remain a viable option for an individual whose freedom is to be
different from a merely natural quality. All of these ideas are to
be found in that impressive monument to the power of Logos
that Hegel erected in his *Science of Logic.* And yet all of these
ideas undercut the power of the Hegelian Logos. For Hegel's

Logos is—or at least it is meant to be—an accomplished unity of knowledge and being. Now from the point of view of knowledge, the option for the blind violence of exclusion is, we saw, profoundly irrational: to *know* myself as being violent in this way amounts to recognize my sameness with (and not difference from) other such violent individuals. But, on the other hand, we have also learned that if man's communal status is not to be another nature to him, then that option for the violence of exclusion—the option for the repudiation of all communal bonds and ties—must remain viable for him. Thus the unity of being and knowledge—and hence also the unity of the Hegelian Logos—is broken wide open; for the very same violence which remains entirely spurious from the standpoint of *knowledge,* imposes its own claim of *being* insofar as it exercises its pull upon individuals searching to assert themselves as capable of an existence independent of all communal bonds and ties. Neither is it the case that the subsequent stages of the *Science of Logic* can remove this threat to the unity of knowledge and being. For those "exclusive," purely destructive, human attitudes are not left behind and safely locked up in a past which cannot return. They remain man's actual options insofar as our rationality can never be frozen into a natural quality of the human self.

NOTES

I.   THE OPENING MOVES

1. Both proposals of course, are to be found in Kant. In the Transcendental Deduction Kant argues for, among other things, the following position: insofar as they are to be *known*, objects must be constructed through mind's imposition of lawfulness upon the originally neutral representations of senses. The object of experience just *is* the (constructed) rule-like connection of a certain group of properties (*CPR* A104–5). Unfortunately, there is no reason at all why the same rule—by its very nature inevitably general—could not account for the behavior of several such objects. Kant's (and especially some neo-Kantians') belief that an object's unique particularity is to be found only at the ideal limit of our cognitive process of determining the object's properties and their connections (the fully determined object is thus a task, an *Aufgabe,* rather than an actual fact) can only be justified if the principle of the identity of indiscernibles is necessarily true; otherwise there is no reason why several objects, even when fully and completely determined as indistinguishable both in their properties and in the law that binds them could still not differ numerically. And no such justification of the principle of the identity of indiscernibles is to be found in Kant. Besides—and here Hegel's standard objection against Kant becomes quite pertinent—such an appeal to an infinite and never-to-be-completed task spells the very opposite for the case(s) at hand: we still lack a satisfying rule for our *actual* identifications of and discriminations between different particulars. There is no difference, in this respect, between what the *Phenomenology of Spirit* criticizes as the "hypocrisies" of Kant's radically dualistic moral philosophy and the case we are now considering. For if our standard is indeed to be found only at that ever-receding limit of the cognitive process, then we cannot take seriously the effectiveness of that standard in assessing and sorting out our actual experiences; conversely, if we continue to rely on our standard in those actual epistemic practices, then the standard itself ceases to be viewed as the term of an infinite and never-to-be-completed task.

As for the doctrines from the Transcendental Aesthetic—where the particularity of things is explained by the uniqueness and exclusivity of their spatial (and temporal) positions—Kant himself abandons these doctrines later on in the *Critique.* Since, as he argues in the Anticipations of Perception, space itself is not an object of a possible experience, the identification of a place must be dependent upon our prior identification of what occupies or fills it. Thus—to take Kant's own, still incomplete view one step further—my ability to discriminate between

places and to establish distances in space presupposes a certain system
of familiar points of reference (cities, mountains, lakes, etc.) with respect to which the organization of space is established. But then the
problem of particulars reappears at once: for if a place is to be distinguished from other places by the item that occupies it we must have
an independent way of identifying that item qua particular, and not just
as a bundle of universal properties (which the item in question could
very well share with others, thereby becoming once again indistinguishable from them). Most philosophers defending the position I
am now describing would quickly reply that there is at least one such
item whose unique particularity is immediately recognized by me—
and that is simply my own body, which thus becomes immediately
capable of furnishing one constant point of reference determining my
grasp of places and distances. The reply is on the right track, but there
remains one outstanding difficulty to be met: one must still supply an
account of just how, and on what grounds, do I come to grasp my body
as an unique particular (and not as a cluster of properties which I share
with others). Now—as I have argued elsewhere (see P. Hoffman, *The
Human Self and the Life and Death Struggle*, chaps. 1 and 3)—if I
identify my body as "mine" immediately and without any use of some
general criteria of identity, it is because, due to my vulnerability and
powerlessness vis-à-vis *the other*, I have a sense that the fate of *this*
particular power center that I am is dependent upon the existence of *this*
body. A threat to my body's existence is a threat to my existence. Hence
my body's Here is unique, for it is *my* Here—were I to think and act
otherwise I know I would be inviting my own annihilation. Let us note
the very special character of this dependence of myself viewed as a
power center upon the life of my body. In effect, we are not dealing here
with a case of a logical necessity (one can at least think of angels or devils
exercising their powers while remaining disembodied); but neither are
we here confronted with just another case of an ordinary matter of fact,
since for a human agent the dependence of his power upon the existence of his body is the sort of "matter of fact" which must be counted
among the very conditions of possibility of his form of life.

2. Thus, in his Fourth Letter to Clarke, Leibniz writes: "to suppose
two things *indiscernible* is to suppose the *same thing* under *two names*"
(G. W. Leibniz, *Letters to Samuel Clarke*, in *Leibniz, Selections*, ed.
Wiener, p. 229). It would seem, then, that the distinction between two
indiscernibles would be merely verbal and, if not altogether meaningless, then at least leading into a logical contradiction were the two
names to be taken as referring to two different things.

3. Ibid, p. 243.
4. Ibid, p. 244.

5. A. J. Ayer, *Philosophical Essays,* (London, 1963), p. 35.

6. G. W. Leibniz, *Letters to Samuel Clarke,* p. 244.

7. P. Hoffman, *Doubt, Time, Violence:* Conclusion.

8. The argument can be traced all the way back to Maine de Biran and Schopenhauer. For its recent eloquent restatement, see Hans Jonas, *The Phenomenon of Life* (New York 1966), pp. 26–33.

9. Norman Kemp Smith, *A Commentary to Kant's "Critique of Pure Reason"* (New York 1962), p. 375.

10. This is the case with P. F. Strawson's well-known interpretation. Because Strawson repudiates Kant's idealistic metaphysics of the transcendental faculties of mind, he can point to a *"non-sequitur* of numbing grossness"* where Kant steps from the necessity in our percep-tions of the objectively succeeding events to an alleged necessity in the causal connection between those objectively succeeding events (P. F. Strawson, *The Bounds of Sense* [London, 1966], p. 137). Conse-quently, when Strawson himself tries to salvage some aspects of the Kantian argument he gives up on Kant's own stringent requirement for causal necessity (ibid. pp. 144–46).

11. Smith, *A Commentary,* pp. 379–80.

12. See Hoffman, *The Human Self and the Life and Death Struggle,* chap 3.

13. A. C. Ewing, *A Short Commentary on Kant's "Critique of Pure Reason"* (Chicago, 1974), p. 218.

14. A. Schopenhauer, *The World as Will and Representation* (New York, 1958), 1: 497–98.

15. Needless to say, Kant was unconvinced by Aquinas's version of the cosmological argument to the effect that a supposition of an infinite series of causes would imply that nothing exists at the present moment.

16. I. Kant, *Religion within the Limits of Reason Alone* (New York, 1960), p. 45n.

17. D. Hume, *A Treatise of Human Nature* (Oxford, 1968), pp. 80–81.

18. L. W. Beck, *A Commentary on Kant's "Critique of Practical Reason"* (Chicago, 1963), p. 184.

19. ". . . the concept of creation does not belong to the sensuous mode of conceiving of existence or to causality but can be referred only to noumena." I. Kant, *Critique of Practical Reason and Other Writings in Moral Philosophy* (Chicago, 1949), p. 207.

20. Ibid., p. 158 (my emphasis).

21. Ibid., p. 159 (my emphasis).

22. P. Hoffman, *The Human Self and the Life and Death Struggle,* chaps. 1 and 2.

23. Cf. especially, in the *Analytic of Principles,* chap. 3, "The Ground

of the Distinction of All Objects in General into Phenomena and Noumena."

24. J. G. Fichte, *Grundlage des Naturrechts nach Prinzipien der Wissenschaftslehre,* in J. G. Fichte, *Sämtliche Werke* (Berlin, 1965), 3: 80–81.

25. I. Kant, *Religion within the Limits of Reason Alone,* Book One, "Concerning the Indwelling of the Evil Principle with the Good, or, On the Radical Evil in Human Nature."

26. See P. Hoffman, *Doubt, Time, Violence.*

27. D. Hume, *A Treatise of Human Nature* (Oxford, 1968), p. 1.

28. Ibid.

29. Ibid., p. 251.

30. Ibid.

31. Ibid., p. 253.

32. Ibid., p. 252.

33. Ibid., p. 253.

34. Ibid., p. 252.

35. Ibid.

36. Ibid., p. 201.

37. Ibid., p. 254.

38. "What I have said concerning the first origin and uncertainty of our notion of identity, as apply'd to the human mind, may be extended with little or no variation to that of *simplicity.* An object, whose different co-existent parts are bound together by a close relation, operates upon the imagination after much the same manner as one perfectly simple and indivisible, and requires not a much greater stretch of thought in order to its conception. From this similarity of operation we attribute a simplicity to it, and feign a principle of union as the support of this simplicity, and the center of all the different parts and qualities of the object." Ibid., p. 263; Cf, too, p. 221.

39. Ibid., p. 261 (my emphasis).

40. Ibid., pp. 109–10.

41. Ibid., p. 109.

42. Barry Stroud, *Hume* (London, 1977), chap. 6.

43. Ibid., p. 125.

44. See Hume, *Treatise,* p. 252.

45. Ibid., p. 260.

46. B. Stroud, *Hume.*

47. Ibid., p. 139.

48. It is worth emphasizing how radical Hume's no-ownership theory is: Hume holds that each and every distinguishable perception could actually exist in separation from a mind. Ibid., p. 207.

49. "Lest my readers should stumble at the alarming evil consequences which may over-hastily be inferred from this statement, I may

remind them that *for thought* the categories are not limited by the conditions of our sensible intuition, but have an unlimited field. It is only the knowledge of that which we think, the determining of the object, that requires intuition" (*CPR* B167 n.).

50. ". . . in the consciousness of myself in mere thought I am the *being itself,* although nothing in myself is thereby given for thought" (*CPR* B429).

51. With this proposition, it is worth noting, we are at the threshold of Fichte's *Wissenschaftslehre.*

52. See especially: SL 776–83; *Enc.* I, #47; *Enc.* III, #378; *Lectures on the History of Philosophy,* 3: 446–48.

53. SL 47; see, too *Lectures on the History of Philosophy,* 3: 450–51.

54. *Enc.* III, #424; *The Phenomenology of Mind,* pp. 211–12.

55. *The Phenomenology of Mind,* p. 219.

56. Ibid., pp. 231–32; cf, too, *Enc.* III, #431.

II.   HEGEL: LOGOS AND VIOLENCE

1. The best treatment of the subject is still to be found in H. F. Fulda, *Das Problem einer Einleitung in Hegels Wissenschaft der Logik* (Frankfurt a/M, 1965).

2. See Hegel, *The Phenomenology of Mind,* Baillie transl. (London, 1966), pp. 805–6. See, too, A. Kojève's explanation of this important point, *Introduction à la lecture de Hegel* (Paris, 1979), pp. 417–21.

3. Here, as in the *Phenomenology* and elsewhere, Hegel is firmly "against method," to use the expression made famous by Paul Feyerabend. See Robert C. Solomon, *In the Spirit of Hegel,* (New York, 1983), chap. 6.

4. "Being, pure being . . . is equal only to itself. It is also not unequal relatively to an other; it has no diversity within itself nor any with a reference outwards. It would not be held fast in its purity if it contained any determination or content which could be distinguished in it or by which it could be distinguished from an other" (SL 80). See also Hegel's own detailed commentary on Parmenides in his *Lectures on the History of Philosophy,* 1: 247–49.

5. In his commentary on Parmenides' poem Hegel quotes the passage where the goddess identifies the road of Being with the road of truth (ibid. p. 252).

6. "*Nothing* is usually opposed to *something;* but the being of *something* is already determined and is distinguished from another *something;* and so therefore the nothing which is opposed to the something is also the nothing of a particular something, a determinate

nothing. Here, however, nothing is to be taken in its indeterminate simplicity . . . nothing, purely on its own account, negation devoid of any relations" (SL 83).

7. See especially his *Sense and Sensibilia* (New York, 1964).

8. Thus Hegel tells us that "being—does not pass over but has passed over—into nothing" (SL 83). In spite of the awkwardness of expression (but could this be avoided at the present early stage?) Hegel's point is clear enough: we cannot identify the moment when being passes over into nothing for being is *always already* on its way to become nothing.

9. E. Fleischmann, *La science universelle ou la logique de Hegel* (Paris, 1968), pp. 67–68, brings out forcefully the identity of *Werden* with the pure object-less process of thinking—without, however, noticing the connection of this process with the underlying existential attitude. According to Hegel, it is the "deep thinking Heraclitus" (SL 83) who must be credited with the discovery of the nontemporal process of pure Logos. See, too, Hegel, *Lectures on the History of Philosophy,* 1:278–93.

10. Plato, *Philebus,* 23c–26e. See, too, Hegel's comments on *Philebus* in *Lectures on the History of Philosophy,* 2:68–70.

11. Here is Hegel's clearest statement to that effect: "Quality . . . although a mode of being, is no longer and immediately identical with being, but a mode indifferent and external to it" (Enc. I, #90, Zusatz).

12. SL 128. This example of Hegel's must be considered in conjunction with Hegel's explanations in the *Philosophy of Nature*'s section on "Space and Time" (Enc. II, pp. 28–44, but especially #256, including its Remark and Zusatz).

13. *Lectures on the Philosophy of Religion,* 1:175.

14. Ibid., pp. 271–72.

15. The *experience* and its contradiction are described in the *Phenomenology of Mind,* pp. 615–41.

16. SL 31. See, too, Jean Hyppolite's beautiful study, *Logique et existence* (Paris, 1953).

17. *The Phenomenology of Mind,* pp. 171–78.

18. SL 148; see, too, A. Koyré, *"Note sur la langue et la terminologie hégéliennes,"* in A. Koyré, *Etudes d'histoire de la pensée philosophique* (Paris, 1971), pp. 195–96.

19. Cf. especially *Enc.* III, ##413–17.

20. *The Phenomenology of Mind* p. 219.

21. Ibid., p. 229; my emphasis.

22. "Monads are the true atoms of nature." Leibniz, *The Monadology,* no. 3.

23. Hegel, *Lectures on the Philosophy of Religion,* (New York, 1974), 1:187–201.

24. Ibid. pp. 183–210.

25. Ibid. p. 189.

26. The striking similarity of Hegel's position with Hobbes's analysis of vanity as the cause of human violence is brought out by Hegel himself. "Hobbes has justly remarked that the true state of nature is a war of every man against his neighbor" (*Lectures on the History of Philosophy,* 2:92); moreover, Hegel points out, for Hobbes this state of warfare is due to the fact that "all [men] possess the desire to rule over one another" (ibid., 3:317), i.e., are inherently vain. Cf., too, Leo Strauss's comments at the end of the French edition of his study *On Tyranny*: L. Strauss, *De la tyrannie* (Paris, 1954), p. 308.

27. Hegel, *Jenenser Realphilosophie, Philosophie des Geistes,* in Sämtliche Werke, (Leipzig, 1932), 20:226–30.

28. "Remark: The Kantian Construction of Matter from the Forces of Attraction and Repulsion" (SL 178–184). I will have more to say on this Remark later on.

29. Hegel, *Reason in History* (Indianapolis, 1953), p. 54.

30. In the state of nature men would lack even the *desire* for freedom (ibid.).

31. Thus Hegel talks about "the reflected vanity of simple, immediate Being-for-itself, of the cold and reserved isolation of the existent "I," which takes up an exclusive attitude towards its Essence, and negates its own essence in itself." *Lectures on the Philosophy of Religion,* 1:216).

32. For all the quotes that follow immediately, see *Lectures on the Philosophy of Religion,* 1:5.

33. Ibid., 3:53.

34. Ibid.

35. In faith, the human self "has an object and this as being the Essence is the absolute Object. It is at the same time no foreign object, no object which is for consciousness something other than and beyond it, but is its own Potentiality, its Essence." Ibid., 1:212.

36. *Hegel's Philosophy of Right* (London, 1967), p. 22.

37. Ibid.

38. "In losing ourselves in the true object, we escape from this vanity of the self-maintaining subjectivity, from this Ego, and make serious work with vanity. *This follows as a consequence of what was accomplished in the science of logic*" Lectures on the Philosophy of Religion, 1:201; my emphasis.

39. The passage is so packed with argument, that I will have to analyze literally every one of its sentences—they are all to be found in the four subsequent notes.

40. "They *are*—this is presupposed in this inter-relatedness—and they *are* only insofar as they reciprocally negate one another and at the

same time hold themselves aloof from this their ideality, their negated-
ness, that is, negate this reciprocal negating." SL 171.

41. "But they *are* only insofar as they negate; consequently, since
this their negating is negated, their being is negated." Ibid.

42. "It is true, that since they *are*, they would not be negated by this
negating, which for them is only something external; this negating by
the other rebounds off them and touches only their surface." Ibid.

43. "And yet it is only through this negating of the others that the
ones return into themselves: they *are* only as this mediation, and this
their return is their self-preservation and their being-for-self." Ibid.

44. This Remark's immediate purpose is to critically comment
upon and deepen the "metaphysical construction" of the concept of
matter devised by Kant as a way of getting around Newton's opposition to the idea of attraction across distance as the essential property of
matter. In the second chapter of his *Metaphysical Foundations of Natural
Science*—the chapter is titled "Metaphysical Foundations of Dynam-
ics"—Kant attempts to demonstrate how the concept of the attractive
force is implied by the very concept of matter as an object of experience.
To be sure, only the repulsive force (impenetrability) is given to us
directly in experience "as the fundamental property of matter whereby
it first reveals itself as something real in the space of our external senses"
(Kant, *Metaphysical Foundations of Natural Science* [Indianapolis and
New York, 1970], p. 56). Nevertheless, it can then be shown by a
purely conceptual analysis how our concept of matter is unintelligible if
taken in separation from the concept of attractive force. Kant's argument is simple: if the force of attraction would not counteract the force
of repulsion, then matter would disperse itself to infinity, and space
would be void of any material objects (ibid., p. 57). We must, therefore, posit the force of attraction as just as necessary to our concept of
matter as is the force of repulsion. The only reason why we find it
difficult to put attraction on an equal footing with repulsion is because
repulsion alone is capable of producing sensation (ibid., p. 59); but this
empirical privilege of repulsion cannot withstand our conceptual analysis. Kant will argue, too, that the attraction he has just shown to be the
necessary component of matter can indeed act at a distance through an
empty space (ibid., pp. 61–62).

The immensely favorable contrast that Hegel draws between Kant
and the (Newtonians') "vulgar mechanistic thinking" (SL 181) is,
however, tempered with three main criticisms whose thrust is, invariably, the same: Kant has stopped half-way between the "external"
(mechanistic) conception of matter and its truly dialectical comprehension. For while the two forces are indeed necessary to the concept of
matter, *their own* relationship, as conceptualized by Kant, is still stained

with the stigma of externality and indifference. The three main criticisms that Hegel advances are as follows:

(1) Kant starts with a mere *perception* of matter and his method is, therefore, distorted by crude empiricism. Had Kant started with a reflection upon the (conceptual) conditions of the possibility of perception he would have seen that the force of attraction must be, and is in fact, just as much present in our experience (for example, Hegel points out, in our experience of cohesion, where parts of a body are immediately felt as attracting each other) as is the force of repulsion (SL 180–81).

(2) In Kant the two forces remain different from and external to each other instead of being viewed as the two aspects of one and the same force: "these forces are only moments which pass over into each other, as we saw above [i.e., in Hegel's own analysis of repulsion and attraction] when they were considered in their truth" (SL 182). For example (SL 183), according to Kant matter can "fill" the space only due to its repelling force, while the force of attraction can only determine matter to "occupy" space. But, Hegel objects, if repulsion thus "fills" the space with a material object made up of several parts (or atoms), and if the relation that exists among these parts is unthinkable without the notion of cohesion (i.e., attraction), then it makes no sense to attribute the capacity to "fill" the space to repulsion alone. Already in the *Phenomenology of Mind* (pp. 183–89) Hegel was expounding on this interchange of functions between the allegedly independent forces; and his analyses in the *Science of Logic* were meant to demonstrate in the element of pure conceptuality how attraction and repulsion pass into each other.

(3) Kant commits a mistake very similar to the mistake we have committed at an earlier stage of the logical development (SL 168), when we interpreted repulsion as taking place between the ones which were already *given* prior to repulsion; the mistake was corrected when we moved on to conceive repulsion in its true function—"in its true Notion" (ibid.)—of actually producing the ones. Similarly, in Kant, both attraction and repulsion are still "represented as forces, not through which matter first comes into being but through which matter, as an already finished product, is only set in motion" (SL 184).

These criticisms are the stepping stones for the predictable conclusion that the application of the Hegelian conception of attraction and repulsion allows us to move further—and towards a more satisfying standpoint—along the road of that "metaphysical" construction of matter that Kant was the first to explore. It is important to stress the *metaphysical* character of these constructions; for it is clear that we are not here dealing with any scientific laws but with a certain body of propositions supplying the broadest framework within which something like the "material world" (as studied by mathematical physics) can first be made intelligible. And, as Hegel sees it, the intelligibility of this world requires the conceptual grid he has brought out in the *Science of Logic.*

Is the claim sound? Are we really convinced that matter is sustained—in its own right and quite independently of human interpretations—by that interplay of attraction and repulsion that Hegel discovered by conceptualizing the paradigm of the human condition? The question involves the complicated issue of the status of the dialectics of nature. I cannot take up this issue here; but, following in the footsteps of some of the most illustrious dialecticians of our century, I tend to think that matter is blind and deaf to the call of dialectics.

45. This theme was pursued at length in the *Phenomenology of Spirit*'s famous section on "Lordship and Bondage": while the courageous master breaks freely the bond of identity with his particular self, the cowardly slave is forced to do so by the ever-present threat of death imposed upon him by the master.

WORKS CITED

Austin, J. L. *Sense and Sensibilia*. New York: Oxford University Press, 1964.

Ayer, A. J. *Philosophical Essays*. London: St. Martin's, 1963.

Beck, L. W. *A Commentary on Kant's "Critique of Practical Reason."* Chicago: University of Chicago Press, 1963.

Ewing, A. C. *A Short Commentary on Kant's "Critique of Pure Reason."* Chicago: University of Chicago Press, 1974.

Fichte, J. G. *Grundlage des Naturrechts nach Prinzipien der Wissenschaftslehre*. In J. G. Fichte, *Sämtliche Werke*. Berlin: Walter de Gruyter, 1965, Vol. 3.

Fleischmann, E. *La science universelle ou la logique de Hegel*. Paris: Plon, 1968.

Fulda, H. F. *Das Problem einer Einleitung in Hegels Wissenschaft der Logik*. Frankfurt a/M: Klostermann, 1965.

Hegel, G. W. F. *Hegel's Logic: Part One of the Encyclopaedia of the Philosophical Sciences*. Oxford: Clarendon Press, 1975.

———.*Hegel's Philosophy of Nature: Part Two of the Enclyclopaedia of the Philosophical Sciences*. Oxford: Clarendon Press, 1970.

———.*Hegel's Philosophy of Mind: Part Three of the Encyclopaedia of the Philosophical Sciences*. Oxford: Clarendon Press, 1971.

———.*Hegel's Philosophy of Right*. London: Oxford University Press, 1967.

———.*Hegel's Science of Logic*. New York: Humanities Press, 1969.

———.*Jenenser Realphilosophie, Philosophie des Geistes*. In *Sämtliche Werke*. Leipzig: Meiner, 1932, vol. 19, pp. 226–230.

———.*Lectures on the History of Philosophy*. New York: Humanities Press, 1974, vols. 1, 2.

———.*Lectures on the Philosophy of Religion*. New York: Humanities Press, 1974, vols. 1, 3.

———.*Reason in History*. Indianapolis: Bobbs-Merrill, 1953.

———.*The Phenomenology of Mind*. New York: Humanities Press, 1966.

Hoffman, P. *The Human Self and the Life and Death Struggle*. Gainesville/Tampa: University Presses of Florida, 1984.

———.*Doubt, Time, Violence*. Chicago: University of Chicago Press, 1986.

Hume, D. *A Treatise of Human Nature*. Oxford: Oxford University Press, 1968.

Hyppolite, J. *Logique et existence*. Paris: Presses Universitaires de France, 1953.

Jonas, H. *The Phenomenon of Life*. New York: Dell, 1966.

Kant, I. *Critique of Pure Reason*. New York: St. Martin's Press, 1965.

———.*Critique of Practical Reason*. In *Critique of Practical Reason and Other Writings in Moral Philosophy*. Chicago: University of Chicago Press, 1949.

———.*Metaphysical Foundations of Natural Science*. Indianapolis and New York: Bobbs-Merrill, 1970.

———.*Religion within the Limits of Reason Alone*. New York: Harper and Row, 1960.

Kemp Smith, N. *A Commentary to Kant's "Critique of Pure Reason."* New York: Humanities Press, 1962.

Kojève, A. *Introduction à la lecture de Hegel*. Paris: Gallimard, 1979.

Koyré, A. "Note sur la langue et la terminologie hégéliennes," in A. Koyré, *Etudes d'histoire de la pensée philosophique*. Paris: Gallimard, 1971.

Leibniz, G. W. *Letters to Samuel Clarke*. In *Leibniz, Selections*, ed. Wiener. New York: Charles Scribner's Sons, 1951.

———.*The Monadology*. In Weiner, *Leibniz, Selections*.

Plato, *Philebus*. In *The Collected Dialogues of Plato*. Princeton: Princeton University Press, 1971.

Schopenhauer, A. *The World as Will and Representation*. New York: Dover, 1958.

Solomon, R. C. *In the Spirit of Hegel*. New York: Oxford University Press, 1983.

Strauss, L. *De la tyrannie*. Paris: Gallimard, 1954.

Strawson, P. F. *The Bounds of Sense*. London: Methuen, 1966.

Stroud, B. *Hume*. London: Routledge and Kegan Paul, 1977.

INDEX

Becoming, pure, 84–85, 93, 104, 110, 117
Being, pure, 78–84, 104, 110; and man's existential attitude, 81–84, 88, 117; and the human condition, 81–84, 104; and human moods and sentiments, 82–84, 88, 104, 145
Body, 152 n. 1

Causality, 10–13, 23, 26–28; and freedom, 26–29; in Kant, 13–26

Death, 84, 104, 119

Evil: and freedom, 50, 132–49; and self, 50, 132–49; in Hegel, 132–49
"Evil demon," in Descartes, vii, 13, 51–52
Exclusion, in Hegel, 131–43, 146–49

Fichte, J. G., 48–49, 105–7
Freedom, 26–28, 41; and creativity, 26–28, 50; and danger, 50; and reason, 50, 51, 135, 148–49; and the other, 27–28; in Kant, 29–50; in Hegel, 132–49

Hobbes, T., vii, 13, 134, 157 n. 26
Husserl, E., 91

Infinity, true and spurious, in Hegel, 108–17

Leibniz, G. W., 5–6, 9–10, 122, 131
Logos, 76–77, 104, 148–49

Machiavelli, N., vii, 13

Nothing, pure, 80–84, 104, 117

Other, the, viii, 6–13, 26–28, 51–52, 152 n. 1; and causal necessi-ty, 10–13, 26–28; and freedom, 26–28; and the principle of the identity of indiscernibles, 5–7; as causal power, 10; in Hegel, 71, 123–49; the threat of, viii, 6–13, 26–28, 51–52, 152 n. 1
Origination. *See* Freedom

Paralogisms, the, in Kant, 63–67
Personal identity, 51–52; in Hegel, 67–71, 119–43; in Hume, 52–59; in Kant, 59–67

Reason, as man's vocation, 97–99. *See also* Freedom; Violence
Recognition, struggle for, 146–48
Repulsion and attraction, in Hegel, 127–43, 158 n. 44; in Kant, 158 n. 44

Self: as enduring and continuing, 51–52; as finite, 83–93; as free, 50, 132–49; as self-consciousness, 71, 120–22. *See also* Personal identity
Strawson, P. F., 153 n. 10
Stroud, B., 57–58

Thing, 1–10; as a bundle of prop-erties, 2–5, 8; as a particular bearer, 2, 6, 8–9

Time, 15–17, 21–22, 43, 66, 85

Violence, vii, 6–13, 23, 26–29, 41, 50–51, 71, 132–40, 143–49; and causality, 10–13, 23, 26; and community, vii, 143–49; and en-during self, 51–52, 71; and free-dom, 26–29, 41, 50; and origination, 26–29, 41, 50; and social conflicts, vii; and reason, 50–51, 135, 149; in Hegel, 71, 132–40, 143–49